IMAGES
of America

MINING IN
BUTTE

IMAGES
of America

MINING IN
BUTTE

World Museum of Mining

ARCADIA
PUBLISHING

Copyright © 2011 by World Museum of Mining
ISBN 978-1-5316-4985-2

Published by Arcadia Publishing
Charleston, South Carolina

Library of Congress Control Number: 2011920139

For all general information, please contact Arcadia Publishing:
Telephone 843-853-2070
Fax 843-853-0044
E-mail sales@arcadiapublishing.com
For customer service and orders:
Toll-Free 1-888-313-2665

Visit us on the Internet at www.arcadiapublishing.com

*To all the miners whose dedication and hard work at
the mines in Butte made the city what it is and enabled
the rich history and legacy we have today*

CONTENTS

ACKNOWLEDGMENTS

The images in this volume appear courtesy of the World Museum of Mining Photograph Archives. In many instances, the name of the original photographer is lost to time. The museum is grateful to the photographers who captured these images.

Executive director Tina Green and curator Dolores Cooney, on behalf of the World Museum of Mining, wish to thank Logan Dudding and Jim Killoy for their significant contributions to this volume.

Thanks also to the dedicated volunteers of the World Museum of Mining Photograph Archives for thei invaluable work on this book and their dedication to preserving the museum's photograph collection: Joe Slouber, Alta Miller, Pat Mohan, Joe Walsh, Monty Duncan, Alice Given, Ted Granvold, Pat Sorich, and Shirley Groff.

Thanks to the following for their contributions to Logan Dudding's research and for their expertise: Paul Bingham, Ed Drabant, Bill and Jane Dudding, Tom Holter, Louis Loushin, Jerry Lynch, Joe Navarro, Will O'Neill, Kevin Shannon, and John T. Shea.

Thank you to Jacqueline Janosko and Courtney McKee for their editing.

INTRODUCTION

There have been many books written about Butte, its people, the mines, and the history. This look at Butte strives to narrow the vast history of mining to three key pieces: the working of the mines, the mine sites, and the people who worked in the mines. To describe even a fraction of the large picture is an immense task. Through photographs, which are part of the World Museum of Mining's vast collection, we present a snapshot of this piece of irreplaceable history.

The photographs contained in this book were produced by many different photographers. Most of their names are lost today. We are eternally indebted to these people whose photographs have preserved history.

The city of Butte was built on mining. At the beginning of the 20th century, there were over 450 mines and close to 100,000 people in Butte. The metropolis supported the miners and the mining industry. The entire city of Butte sits on registered mining claims that overlap and cover the entire area. Many of these claims developed into operating mines. Some were small, but others were large mining complexes under the control of a handful of owners.

The evolution of the mines—from the rudimentary use of the whim and the windlass to the steel headframe, which towered over the mine yards—is a story unto itself. The working of the underground mine involved many men, each of whom performed a necessary function in the overall process of extracting the valuable ore from the ground. Many of us will never experience the work that was done underground. The only light the miners had was that which came from the lamp attached to their hardhat. In the early days of mining, candles were the miners' only source of light.

The many mines that dotted the Butte Hill bore the names of faraway places, famous battles, and people and dreams of the original mine locators. The origins of many of the names are lost today. The list of mine names presents us with a reminder of this past. The photographs of the mines and the mine complexes contained in this book are a reminder to those that remember mining in the city and an introduction to those who never saw such a sight.

The snapshot of the people in the mines contained in Chapter Three shows us just some of the dedicated, hard working individuals from the mines. From the group shots of miners from the past to some of the family teams that worked the mines, these photographs show the faces of the men involved a dangerous and hard job.

The World Museum of Mining is pleased to present this small piece of Butte's mines and miners. The book is dedicated to all of these individuals. Over 2,500 men lost their lives in the Butte Mines. A Miner's Memorial bearing the names of these men sits on the grounds of the World Museum of Mining.

MINES ON THE BUTTE HILL. The mines, shown in the 1940s, from left to right, are St. Lawrence Mine, Moonlight Mine, St. Lawrence No. 7 Mine, Anaconda Mine South Shaft, Neversweat Mine, Molloy Murphy Mine, and Anaconda Mine. These mines were just to the north of Park Street above what was then called Finn Town. Much of this area was cleared to make way for the expansion of the Berkeley Pit.

One

WORKING THE MINES

BUTTE, MONTANA, 1875. The white building in the center of the picture is the Hotel DeMineral. The earliest records of settling Butte date back to the spring of 1856, when whites would meet and trade peacefully with Native American tribes. A shallow trench was discovered; it had been carved into the earth by the elk antlers lying nearby. The trench exposed a quartz lode, an indication to the Western prospectors of placer (surface) gold. They discovered an outcropping, which is a mineral or ore deposit that is visible on surface but may, with any luck, trend hundreds or thousands of feet below the earth. This ventured a promise to the prospectors that there could be mineral wealth below the ground.

OLD PROSPECTOR WITH GOLD PAN. The earliest mining in Butte was all conducted on the surface. Prospectors would dig into the ground with shovels, fill buckets with the dirt, and bring them to a nearby creek to pan out the gold. The miners would totally submerge a dirt-filled pan and shake it back and forth, causing the heavier, most valuable materials such as gold to work their way to the bottom; the lighter, worthless materials would wash downstream. The first notable prospectors in Butte were William Allison and G.O. Humphreys. In the spring of 1864, they found their way to the Butte area from the south, traveling from Virginia City, Montana. Alison and Humphreys originally named the area now known as Butte, Baboon Gulch. One morning as the sun peaked over a mountain range, the light reflecting off the creek water gave the appearance of tiny silver bows dancing downstream; naturally, the creek was named, Silver Bow Creek, a name eventually bestowed on the county encompassing Butte.

ORPHAN GIRL MINE, C. 1970. Other placer mining methods were used in Butte. These all had similar origins but varied in their technique. Rocker boxes were filled with dirt and set into the creek. As the water passed through, the box was rocked, similar to a baby cradle, allowing the heavier materials to settle at the bottom. Sluice boxes were similar in design to the rocker boxes but they contained a coarse, carpet-like material designed to trap the heavier materials while allowing the lighter to wash away. Traditional placer mining sprayed high-pressure water on the surface, using gravity to wash the earth to a lower point where it would be collected, panned, rocked, or sluiced. This required a tremendous amount of water pressure, and streams would often have to be redirected to build up enough head pressure to wash away the earth.

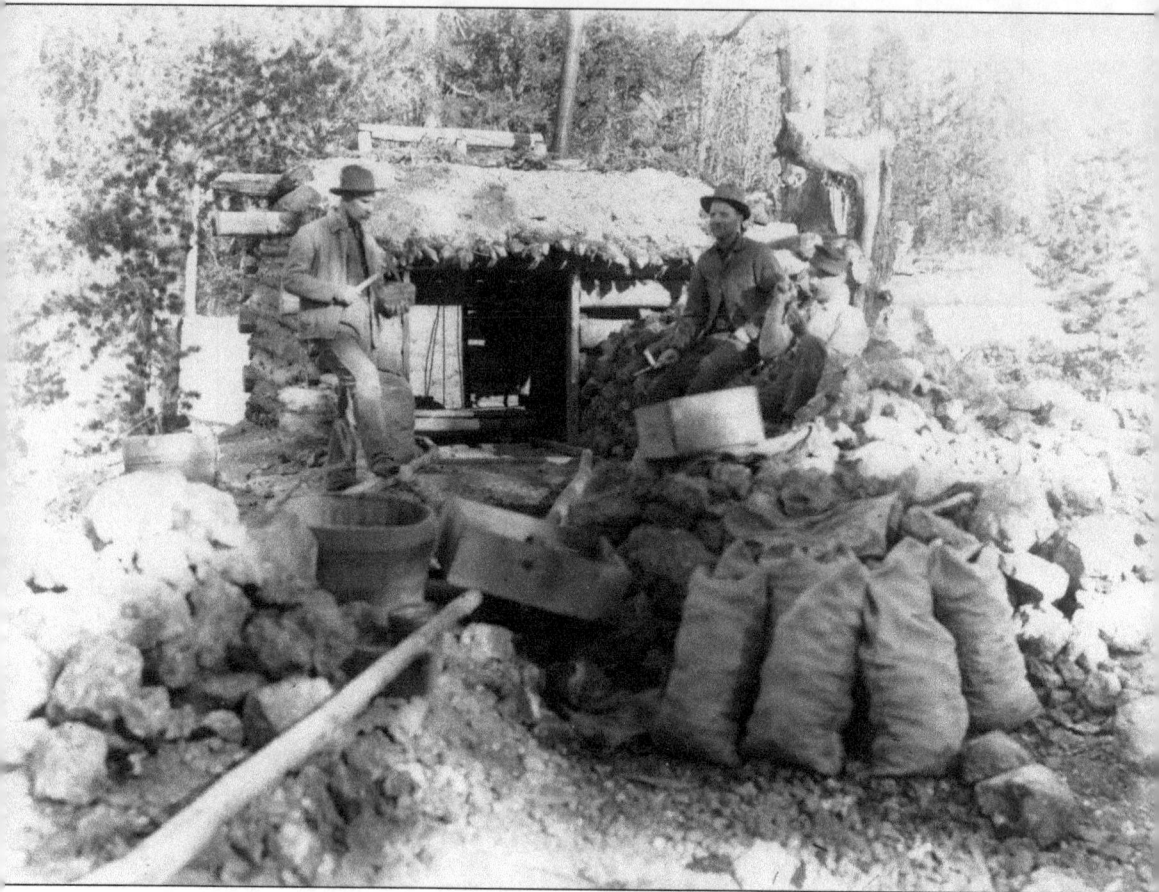

MINE TUNNEL WITH ORE SAMPLES. These ore samples were to be assayed at an East Ridge mine. By 1869, most of the placer gold in and around the Butte area was exhausted, making it all but a ghost town. The 1870s marched in with a new metal commodity, and the lustrous shine of silver brought a fresh wave of prospectors to the area. But silver was not on the ground or in shallow areas in the topsoil. It laid in veins and ore bodies, ranging from a few feet to several hundred feet below the surface.

CLARKS FRACTION MINE, WALKERVILLE. The prospectors became miners. The silver rush sparked the interest of William Andrews Clark, a banker from Deer Lodge Montana. Clark funded a few mining operations by loaning money. When prospectors could not repay their loans, Clark repossessed the claims for himself. Word of the silver boom in Butte made its way down to Salt Lake City, Utah, and into the ears of investment bankers the Walker brothers. The brothers sent Irish immigrant Marcus Daly with the intention of purchasing shares in a silver-producing mine named the Alice. The Walkers and Daly bought majority shares in the Alice. Soon after, while the Alice was producing silver, Daly took a tour of another small claim. One afternoon in the late 1870s, Daly was summoned down 300 feet below the ground of his new mine, the Anaconda Mine. Daly was called because his miners had blasted into a new, black material they had never seen before. As miners shoved explosives in holes that had been drilled into the rock and detonated them, Daly witnessed the blast.

MINERS UNDERGROUND READYING TO BLAST. When the dust settled, Daly picked up a chunk of the new material, examined it, and is believed to have said, "No one knows it yet, but we're standing on the richest hill on earth." Daly was known to have a nose for ore and the black chunk he held in his hand was a copper ore known as chalcocite. At this point in history, copper was mainly a nuisance to miners; it was typically used for pots, pans, and dishes as it held its temperature so well. Copper smelters were nonexistent in the United States. The only place in the world suited to chemically process copper ore was Swansea, Whales. So the earliest copper ores mined in Butte were hand-separated underground by the miners, hoisted to surface, loaded into wagon cars, pulled to Salt Lake City Utah, loaded onto a train, railed to the East Coast, and shipped to Swansea. It became apparent that a copper smelter near Butte was imperative. The only trouble was that copper was useless to an investor.

14

ANACONDA SMELTER, MONTANA. Marcus Daly, a copper king, was fond of saying, "You gotta look to the future," and with some persuasion, San Francisco investors funded his copper smelter to the tune of three million dollars in 1883. The smelter was built 27 miles west of Butte, and although the distance was significant, the water required to concentrate the copper was not available closer, as all of Silver Bow Creek had long since been claimed.

BAP ORE TRAIN. The Butte, Anaconda & Pacific Railway (BAP) would soon connect Butte with Anaconda to transport ore from the mines to the smelter. In the latter half of the 1880s and the early 1890s, copper would boom. The Industrial Revolution along with inventions such as the light bulb, telephone, and telegraph and innovations such as indoor plumbing lead to the explosion in copper. Butte was uniquely positioned to benefit from these new technologies, seated atop a mountain of copper ore with a modern copper smelter ready to produce.

THE HAND WINDLASS. A shaft is a vertical opening into the earth that serves as the primary source for entry, equipment delivery, ore removal, and ventilation of the mine. Mineshafts were started by excavating with a pick and shovel, but once the miners had passed the topsoil layer, drilling holes, filling them with explosives, and blasting was the only method that could be used to advance. The hand windlass was one of the earliest and most primitive sources of hoisting.

THE WHIM. As shaft depths increased, the loads were far too great for any one man to hoist the buckets. Animals were needed to hoist the men, supplies, and rock to the surface. The windlass would be removed and a whim would be constructed in its place. The whim was a long wooden plank or pole attached to a yoke drawn by a horse, mule, or donkey. The animal would walk around in a circle to wrap the rope around the whim lowering and raising the bucket.

THE STEWARD MINE. At the time, this mine belonged to W.A. Clark. The volume of rock being hoisted to surface combined with an ever increasing shaft depth would exhaust an animal after a short period. When this happened, the whim was removed and a wooden headframe would take its place. The headframe had pulley wheels at the top known as sheave wheels; they guided the ropes that hoisted the loads up and down the shaft. Replacing the whim with the headframe also necessitated sturdier buckets. Cages, larger gated metal boxes, were used in their place. Loaded ore cars could be secured and lifted out of the mine in cages. The weight from the cages and cars could be close to 5 tons, and the hoist could lower the cages to depths of several hundred to nearly a thousand feet. Pictured is a two-compartment shaft with an old flat-cable steam hoist; the compartment on the left has a cage with ore cars loaded on each deck, while the right compartment is just the cage.

THE ALICE MINE. Mr. Buzzo, the manager of the mine, is in the center of picture. Some of the earliest headframes were completely enclosed inside of a building known as the lift house. The ground water would soak the miners and having an enclosed headframe kept them out of the elements, making for a better walk home after surfacing from their shifts. A typical winter day in Butte, Montana, could be 50 degrees below zero, and the lift houses kept the surface workers, known as top-landers, out of the harsh conditions. The one major drawback to an enclosed headframe was the threat of fire. For some mines in Butte, the only way in and out and the primary source of ventilation of a mine was a single shaft; carbon monoxide would billow down the shaft if the lift house caught fire.

KELLEY MINE

THE KELLEY MINE, C. 1952. Loads and depths were always increasing in the Butte mines. Shafts were an average of 3,000 feet deep with some reaching 4,000 and 5,000 feet. Loads ranged from three to ten tons, so a small, wooden headframe could not accommodate for such conditions. The smaller headframes were removed and replaced with taller and stronger iron headframes. The Kelley headframe stands 200 feet tall, dwarfing the 100-foot headframe next to it. The straight iron towers behind the tall headframe are idler towers, which used smaller sheave wheels to keep the slacked, downward bow out of the cables. Slack in the cables would cause the cage to bounce inside the shaft and take several minutes to come to rest. Idler towers were needed when the hoists were a great enough distance from the headframe. To most Butte natives, the headframes are known as gallus frames, thought to have been a derivative of the term *gallows frame* in reference to their visual similarity.

19

THE GAGNON AND ORIGINAL MINES. The evolution of the word *gallows* to the word *gallus* is believed to have occurred through the broken English of the wide array of immigrants found in the mines of Butte. The no-smoking signs in the Butte mines were in 16 different languages. Some mine owners favored pairing miners of different nationalities underground, to ensure no talking, only work.

ANSELMO MINE HEADFRAME. Like this structure, which is being erected on June 3, 1936, headframes, idler towers, and steel-structured buildings were all constructed by Butte iron workers. The iron gang constantly had work, as shafts were being closed or upgraded, and the frames were removed and placed elsewhere. Fastened together by hot rivets, they were designed to be dismantled and rebuilt over a different shaft. Most of the iron headframes still standing in Butte stood over a different shaft at one time.

COMPRESSED AIR-GEARED HOIST. These hoists were often used in the small mines as main hoists and in the bigger mines for sinking shafts. When headframes were constructed over a shaft, a more practical means of hoisting was needed to handle the depth and weights. Hoisting systems were installed in front of the headframes to support the demand. Drum-type hoists were favored in Butte, as they would rotate to take in and let out cable.

ANSELMO MINE HOIST. The hoist engineer operates the hoist at the mine on North Excelsior Street. Most mines operated with a three-hoist system using a set of double drums and a single drum. Drums always rotated in the same direction, but one cable would be taken in and the other out. The drums were not limited, as the hoisting engineer could un-clutch each drum and operate them one at a time. Acidic mine water unearthed from the Butte mines could destroy these steel cables. The cables were tarred to repel the mine water and avoid loss.

THE HIGH ORE MINE. Leo Mock is the ropeman rewinding the flat cable on the hoisting engine. Some cables were not round, but instead flat; they were made of inter-woven strands of metal. The flat cables did not have the stretch that a round cable had, making travel harsher. They were also much more likely to shear than a round cable.

EMMA MINE HOISTING ENGINE. This was one of the last hoists in Butte to use flat cable. The earliest hoists were powered by steam. The steam hoists were converted to air power or pneumatic and eventually to electric power. Telephones were not used to communicate from the hoists to the men underground, as the engineer needed two hands to operate the hoist controls, and the noise generated made it nearly impossible to hear.

EMMA MINE HOIST ENGINEER AND OILER. There were no video cameras during these days. The only two indicators of where the cage hung in the shaft was a spin dial that pointed to a specific level indicating shaft depth, but it was only a rough estimate, not an exact indicator. The drum itself had markings that pointed to each level, and it was color-coordinated to show which deck of the cage was even with the level at that time. Most engineers could spot the deck perfectly with the level.

MINERS IN THE DRY. The building containing the hoists was known as the engine room and later on as a hoist house. In addition to the hoist house was a change house known as the dry, home to the showers and locker rooms. When the miners surfaced, they would be soaking wet from water used to settle dust while drilling and the ever present ground water, and they were covered in machine grease. Most miners would step into the shower fully clad in their diggers, or work clothes.

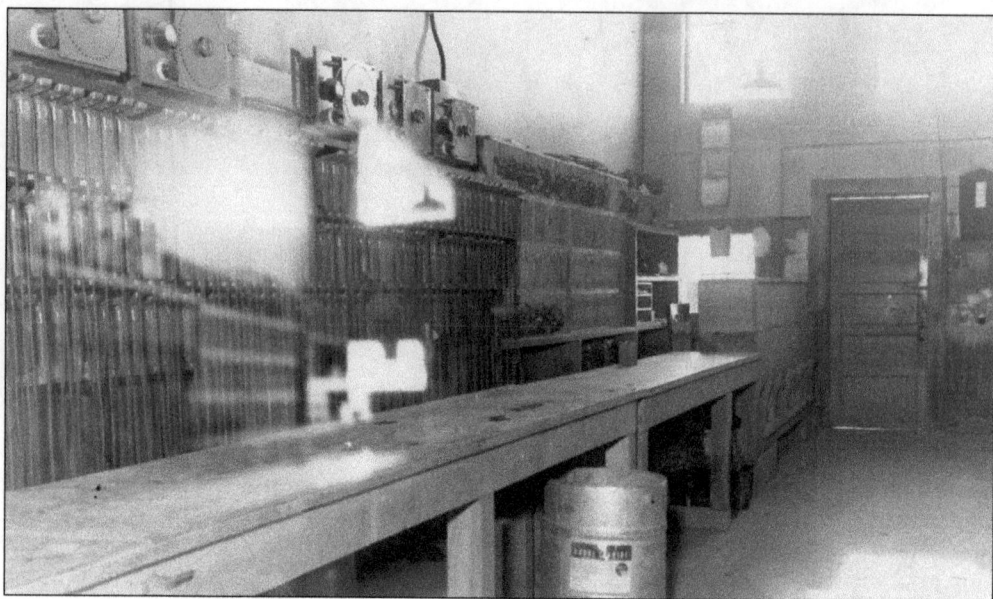

A MINE LAMP ROOM. The hoist house had a lamp room that was a charging station for the head lamps used underground. The miners were issued a lamp in this room at the beginning of their shifts, and returned it at the end of their shifts to be charged for the next day.

APPLYING FIRST AIDE

MINERS APPLYING FIRST AID. Before a miner went underground, he would place a brass tag printed with his last name and specific number on a board; this indicated he was underground. Another brass tag was kept on his person for identification if he was injured or killed during a shift. When the shift was over, he would place his tag on a separate board, indicating he was out of the mine. And if any tags were left on the in side, a shift boss would know to go searching for the missing miner.

THE GREEN MOUNTAIN MINE. The wooden gallows frames were all enclosed at this time. The cables that were cast and reeled by the hoists were attached to cages. Often called chippie cages around Butte, they were similar to elevators. The word *chippie* was also another name for a prostitute, running around catching all of the men.

TWO-DECK COMBINATION AT BUTTE MINE. The cages were stacked on top of each other with anywhere from two to four decks. The decks had rails set in the middle of them to guide ore, powder, water, and timber cars onto each one. Each deck could tightly fit seven men. Horseplay was common on the cage. Veteran miners would kick shins, pull hair, bite, and play other antics on novice miners.

SHAFT COLLAR OF STEWARD MINE. Skips were a long, slender boxes and a practical way to hoist rock and ore out of the mines. The cages traveled in the shaft at 800 feet per minute, which was known as man speed; the skips traveled between 1,500 and 2,800 feet per minute, or rock speed. A single cage was kept at the top of the skip for men to travel with the loads. The Steward Mine had an extra skip.

MINERS, MOUNTAIN CONSOLIDATED MINE. At the beginning of each shift, all three compartments of the shaft were equipped with cages. It could take 45 minutes to 2.5 hours before all miners were below ground. Once the miners were underground, the two cages attached to the double-motor drums were removed and replaced with skips. The third single drum would remain with the cage, lowering supplies.

DANGEROUS WAY TO THE STATION. With the cage bar up, the car can roll off the cage and kill the station tender. Ore was brought out of the Butte mines, mainly by two methods. All of the rock mined was loaded into one-ton, three-ton, five-ton, or ten-ton ore cars. The one-ton cars were small enough to be wheeled on to the cage and hoisted to the surface.

BEFORE THE WORLD MUSEUM OF MINING. Eventually, the Orphan Girl Mine became the home of the World Museum of Mining. Many mine timbers are pictured. The cages were brought up past ground level, through the floor of a house attached to the backside of the headframe. This was the ore house, where the cars were then pulled from the cage.

27

STATION TENDERS LOADING SKIP. Skips were loaded by dumping the contents of the mine car into the skip in the shaft. The top landers would pull a locking pin in the front of the ore car and push it towards a stopping bar. Once the car hit the bar, the box would rotate upwards, dumping its contents into a giant ore bin while all four of its wheels remained on the floor.

MOUNTAIN CON MINE ORE BINS. Copper ore is being loaded for shipment to the Anaconda Smelter around 1940. The ore remained in the bins until a standard-size railcar was motored underneath, filled with the ore, and railed to the Anaconda smelter.

ORE DUMPED INTO POCKET, C. 1950. The bigger ore cars were far too large and heavy to be pushed onto the cage; instead, they were dumped underground. These larger ore cars, referred to as Granby cars, were equipped with a fifth wheel, or trunnion wheel, which was the lever to dump the load. As the wheel reached the top of the camel back, the box rotated sideways, dumping its contents. As the wheel descended the other side, the box returned to center.

MINE CARS IN SHAFT. At the front of the train is a storage battery locomotive. The ore in the mine cars was dumped into 100-foot-deep pockets known as skip pockets. Eventually, the ore filled the skips inside of the shaft, and the rock was hoisted to surface. When it reached daylight, the load was hoisted to the top of the headframe where the skip, equipped with its own set of trunnions, would dump ore into the bins.

THE TIMBER STORAGE DEPOT UNDERGROUND. As drifts, crosscuts, raises, shafts, and stopes were drilled and blasted beneath the earth, the threat of falling rocks became a constant concern. The oldest and most common method of shoring in the Butte mines was square-set timbering. After each blast was mucked out, the miners would line the ceiling and the walls with timbers, which became the back and ribs of the mine.

MINERS READYING TO BLAST. The fuse is timed and ready to fire. Square-set methods consisted of three main timbers. Two posts (typically eight feet in length) were placed vertically, and between the two vertical posts, caps (close to six feet in length) were wedged perpendicular to the direction of travel in a drift. Girts (close to five and a half feet in length) were wedged in between the posts parallel to the direction of travel.

CAVE, ELM ORLU MINE. All timbers were wedged in place without fasteners. The use of nails would be impractical as the acidic mine water could dissolve the metal nails, resulting in the timber sets toppling over.

MINER DRAGGING TIMBER. The posts, caps, and girts all had notches sawn out of the ends, allowing the timbers to lock into each other. The posts had one square end that was placed on the floor of the drift. The only flat boards used were called lagging and were wedged between the caps and back, while two-inch-thick gob lagging was wedged between the posts and ribs. The saying, "Behind the gob," became common lingo among miners; it was a good place to store garbage, tools, waste rock, and sometimes ore if the miners were close to the end of their shift and did not have their area mucked out.

GAGNON MINE MILLING PLANT, C. 1905. The framing timber was completed in Rocker, Montana, and then delivered to the mines. When the Anaconda Company was in full-swing during the 1920s, their mines used over 40,000 board feet per day.

MOUNTAIN CON MINE TIMBER YARD. The company owned saw mills throughout Montana and forest rights to the entire state. In later years, the invention of rock bolts would take the place of timbers in certain areas of the mines.

USING ROCK BOLTS UNDERGROUND. A typical rock bolt for the older days of Butte was a long metal rod, similar to rebar. First, a hole was drilled into the desired location. A driver bit, which is similar to a socket wrench, was placed in the drill to drive the bolt in place. The bolts were placed through a small wooden board, known as a headboard. Headboards helped ensure the bolt was not driven in too far and held the mesh in place.

LEONARD MINE SHAFT. This view looks up from the 800-foot level. Shafts were the primary source of entry into the mines of Butte. They were cribbed in place using 10-to-12-inch-thick posts and caps, notched and wedged the same as a square set, with a pair of guides bolted on each side of the compartment.

EMMA MINE'S BOTTOM SUMP SKIP. The station tender rode above this skip at most of the mines. The cages and skips had troughs or shoes on both sides, which hugged around the guides to keep them straight and on track while traveling. The wood for the guides was not native to Montana, not even to the United States. Guides bore tremendous weight from the cages and skips and endured so much friction that they had to be made of imported hardwood. The guides were generally made from Indonesian Teak or South American Mahogany. The smell of burnt wood was familiar as the cages and skips screamed by. The guides would sever, strip out of their bolts, or get pushed out of alignment quite often, causing danger for the men riding in the cage.

SAFETY DOGS ON CAGES, STEWARD MINE. When a cage or skip would slam into a broken guide, it would no longer move in the shaft. The lingo was, "There is a wreck in the shaft," or "The cage is in the woods." Occupants of the cage could pull a radio bell that dispatched a signal to the engineer indicating the cage stalled. A second cage would be lowered alongside the wrecked cage, allowing riders to exit and be hoisted elsewhere. When this occurred, ropemen were lowered to the stopped cage. It was their job to guide the slack out of the cable. When it slacked, the cable would bend, twist, and form loops or eyes. If the engineer tried to reel in the slack, the eyes would cause the cable strands to unravel, rendering it useless. The rope gang placed short, wooden stulls through the eyes. As slack was drawn in, the cable would snap straight, leaving it intact. Next, the shaft crew would head down next and replace the broken guides.

UNDERGROUND STATION IN MINE.
A shaft station is where the drift
meets the shaft at each level and
where miners would enter and exit
the cage. The stations were larger
than a typical drift to accommodate
groups of miners waiting for the cage
as their shift ended. Many antics
took place while they waited. Some
miners would nail another miner's
rain coat or lunch bucket down.

**GRANITE MOUNTAIN MINE,
3,200-FOOT LEVEL.** This image
shows two hoisting compartments;
the one on the right is the chippie
hoist with a miner standing near
a pocket around 1919. At all shaft
stations, the floors were lined with
metal sheets, making it possible to
wheel and turn the cars without
the use of tracks, but the cars would
be guided on to tracks for travel
down the drift. Station tending was
another occupation in the mine.

CODE OF MINE SIGNALS. When a cage or skip was needed, the station tenders would ring a specific bell code, which was heard by the hoisting engineer; it indicated the level where the cage or skip was needed. Station tenders helped lower and raise the miners during the shift changes, but the duration of their shift was used to roll loaded ore cars onto cages, or open pockets to fill skips. Pockets were opened from the station by strong-arm doors, and in later years, by an air piston. The strong-arm doors were controlled by a chain looped around two sprockets, while air-piston doors were opened easily by pulling a lever. Station tenders were the only men allowed to ring the bells, unless a piece of equipment was too large for the tenders to handle. In that case, rope men would ring the bells. The rope gang was responsible for changing the cages and skips during the shift and often worked with the iron gang. Butte's rope and iron gangs were world-renowned for their craftsmanship, as all the workers of the Butte mines were known as the best.

CODE OF MINE SIGNALS

SHAFT BELLS AND BUZZER SIGNALS FOR HOISTING ENGINEERS

NO ONE IS ALLOWED TO RING SHAFT BELLS EXCEPT STATION TENDERS, SUPERVISORS OR OTHER AUTHORIZED PERSONNEL

5 Bells: Caution.	2 Slow Bells: Lower slowly.
3 Bells: Hoist men to surface.	2-1-2: Clear Signal-Send cage to surface or back to station tenders.
1 Bell (pause) 3 Bells: Hoist station tenders to surface.	1-2: Hoist 1 deck of cage.
3 Slow Bells (pause between): Hoist slowly.	2-1: Lower 1 deck of cage.
1 Bell: Stop cage in motion.	1-2-1: Spot opposite end of cage at level.
2 Bells: Lower men to station tender.	

To move cage or skip to another level: Always use the full station signal.

To hang cage on chair: Ring proper signal to lower or hoist one deck; when cage starts to move, ring 2-2-2 bells; engineer will spot the deck a little high and then lower slowly onto the chair; when the cage rests on the chair, ring 1 long bell; engineer will let out enough slack to allow for cable stretch.

STATION BELLS OR BUZZER SIGNALS FOR LEVELS TO 5000

Bells or Buzzer Signal	Pause	Bells or Buzzer Signal	Station	Bells or Buzzer Signal	Pause	Bells or Buzzer Signal	Station
2	"	1	100	7	"	1	2600
2	"	2	200	7	"	2	2700
2	"	3	300	7	"	3	2800
2	"	4	400	7	"	4	2900
2	"	5	500	7	"	5	3000
3	"	1	600	8	"	1	3100
3	"	2	700	8	"	2	3200
3	"	3	800	8	"	3	3300
3	"	4	900	8	"	4	3400
3	"	5	1000	8	"	5	3500
4	"	1	1100	9	"	1	3600
4	"	2	1200	9	"	2	3700
4	"	3	1300	9	"	3	3800
4	"	4	1400	9	"	4	3900
4	"	5	1500	9	"	5	4000
5	"	1	1600	10	"	1	4100
5	"	2	1700	10	"	2	4200
5	"	3	1800	10	"	3	4300
5	"	4	1900	10	"	4	4400
5	"	5	2000	10	"	5	4500
6	"	1	2100	11	"	1	4600
6	"	2	2200	11	"	2	4700
6	"	3	2300	11	"	3	4800
6	"	4	2400	11	"	4	4900
6	"	5	2500	11	"	5	5000

TO GO ON TOP—OR MOVE TO ANOTHER LEVEL

Flash signal for level on which you are, using the call buzzer signal according to the sign posted by . Always flash for auxiliary cage if the mine has one.

To call auxiliary cage—flash 2 buzzes, follow with station signal.

To call main hoist cage—flash 2 on buzzer.

Station tender will answer with 1 buzz.

Reply—1 buzz to go up. Reply—2 buzzes to go down. Reply—3 buzzes to go to surface.

If you receive a signal reply of 5 buzzes, it means that the station tenders are busy and cannot come immediately.

If you receive a 2-1-2 buzzer signal in reply, this means the station tender or engineer did not get your signal.—Repeat your signal.

If station or skip pocket is full of ore, buzz station signal for main hoist cage, wait for answer (1 buzz) but do not reply.

If station or skip pocket is full of waste, buzz station signal for main hoist cage, wait for answer (1 buzz), reply 4-2-2 on buzzer.

IN CASE OF DANGER OR ACCIDENT

Flash for auxiliary cage by buzzing station signal. When you receive 1 buzz in reply, flash 9 buzzes.

If you cannot get an answer to your flash for the auxiliary cage, buzz for the main hoist cage in the same manner.

Posted at the direction of the Industrial Accident Board of Montana.

Approved By **INDUSTRIAL ACCIDENT BOARD**

Rock Hitting the Chute. The dangerous practice of rock hitting the chute could smash a miner's hand. The earliest form of hauling ore in the mines was pushing loaded ore by hand. It probably took two or three men to get an ore car moving, but once momentum took over, a single miner could shove the great loads down a drift. Hand tramming was the only means of ore hauling until the mid-1880s, when a Butte veterinarian's ideas to use mules changed everything.

Mule Train, Rarus Mine 1,100-Foot Level. Mules were used in Butte mines until electricity was introduced. The last mule was taken from the Emma Mine in 1937. A sling capable of hoisting mules and horses down the shafts had to be invented. Underground stables were constructed to house the mules when they were not pulling. The mules were only brought back to the surface when the mine was being closed, during a lengthy labor strike, or if the mule had become lame and could no longer work.

ORIGINAL MINE HORSE-PULLED CAR, C. 1910. Whereas a man could push only a single car, an average mule could pull five loaded cars. If a mule's cars were being loaded from an ore chute, the mule knew how far away from the chute he stood, and knew when he was loaded with his desired amount of cars. The ore cars made a clicking sound as they were coupled, if the mule had heard one too many clicks; it would not move until the extra car was unlatched. The man responsible for guiding the animal was a muleskinner and his partner, whose job was to clean up the mule waste, was a swamper. The mules had an average life-span of five years underground. By the early teens, the mules had started to be replaced with pneumatic locomotives. The locomotives had an air-receiver tank that stored compressed air to power the motor down on the tracks. Some tools and equipment used by miners were pneumatic, and metal airlines were hung through every drift. If the motor started to lose power, the motorman could refill the receiver at a nearby valve on the airline.

STORAGE BATTERY LOCOMOTIVE. During the 1920s, electric, battery-powered locomotives replaced pneumatic locomotives were. Charging stations or motor barns replaced the mule stables. Similar to the miner's headlamp charging stations, these motor barns housed the motors not in use, allowing them to charge underground. Eventually, the electric motors became so large and powerful that they could pull a handful of three, five, or even ten ton ore cars.

ELECTRIC MOTORS UNDERGROUND. Electric motors were used to charge batteries in the mine. Every active level had at least three motors—one for each of the eight-hour shifts—as ore was hauled 24 hours a day. If a level produced sufficient ore to necessitate two locomotives per shift, six motors would be placed on that level. Motor barns were equipped with a small ceiling crane to change out dead batteries, as some could weigh thousands of pounds.

TURNOUT AT UNDERGROUND MINE. A drift is a mining tunnel. The drifts are typically six feet wide and eight feet tall because the timbers were close to eight feet in length and the caps nearly six feet in length. Drifts were usually spaced 100 vertical feet apart from each other underground, but that distance could be increased, depending on rock strength and ore content. Most mines would not have levels any closer than 100 feet to ensure stability between the levels.

THREE-WAY TURNAROUND UNDERGROUND. Note the keg for water. Trolley wire is overhead in the box for protection. The two different types of drifts driven into the Butte mines were haulage drifts and crosscut drifts. Haulage drifts were the main drifts meeting up with the shaft stations and were rarely, if ever, mined out for ore. The haulage drifts were generally driven parallel with the ore bodies and were treated as underground highway systems. Crosscut drifts branched from the haulage drifts into the ore body.

41

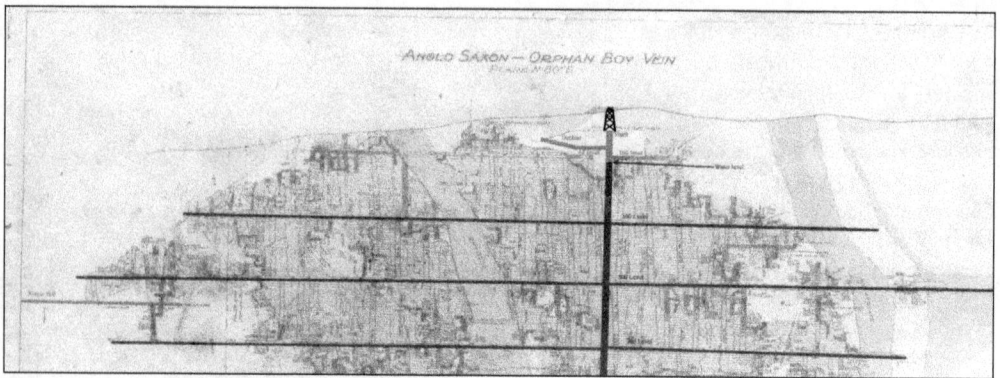

ANGLO SAXON — ORPHAN BOY VEIN

ANGLO SAXON AND ORPHAN BOY VEIN. When mining a level, the ore was usually visible and had the appearance of a vein, which could trend several thousand feet above and below a miner, thus the term *ore body*. Drawings were made of all ore veins. Also, all shaft and drift work was surveyed to guide the mining process and record the mine information. There are over 10,000 miles of tunnels and shafts under Butte today, and the records of this complex system still exist.

GRANITE MOUNTAIN MINE. Miners are cleaning up after a small cave-in. The miners refer to this type of caving as "as slough of ground," shown around 1919. The earliest drifts were hand-mucked with a shovel. After a blast, the muckers were not shoveling dirt or gravel, but larger rocks anywhere from a few inches to a couple feet diameter. These rocks were primarily made of ore, and being metal, the ore outweighed rock dramatically.

MUCKING MACHINE UNDERGROUND, ANSELMO MINE. By the 1920s, a mucking machine, which decreased the need for shovels and sped up the mucking process, had been invented. The mucking machine moved along the tracks, powered pneumatically, pulling an ore car behind it. The miner stood to the side of the machine operating the controls. The bucket would flip backwards, dumping its contents into the ore car behind. The buckets did not ease back into the car, but whipped back quickly and had the potential to decapitate the operator.

LOADING CAR IN DRIFT. Many miners were crushed or killed when the mucking machine tipped over on them. In later years, the machines were equipped with a footboard so a miner could ride it instead of walking. Miners hated these mucking machines in the early days, as there was a sense of pride in mucking the rock with a shovel, and they feared it would replace their job.

UNDERGROUND TIMBER SLIDE WITH ROPE. A raise is a vertical or near-vertical passageway that would connect two different levels together. Since the levels were usually spaced 100 feet apart, the raises had to be 100 feet tall to adjoin the levels. However, it was not unheard of to have a span stretch 200 or even 300 feet if the levels were that far apart. The ropes were used to hoist the mine timbers. A worker climbs the ladder at the left.

SAFELY HOISTING TIMBER. A chain and the safety dog are used to get the timber the stope safely. The miner keeps himself open to be able to step clear if needed. In the Butte mines, raises generally consisted of a manway and an ore chute compartment. The manway had a ladder and a timber slide, which was a little partition to hoist timbers separately from the manway. In addition to being very dangerous for miners, hoisting timbers in the manway could destroy landings between ladder sections.

DANGEROUS MINE CAR LOADING. The second compartment is the ore chute where ore could be mucked from above down to a lower level. The raises were driven upwards from a lower level to the next one above and worked from the bottom up to allow gravity to bring the blasted material down the drift so the rock did not have to be mucked from the top.

GRANITE MOUNTAIN OR SPECULATOR MANWAY. As raises were advanced, they were cribbed similar to shafts. Raises were commonly six-feet-wide timbers and wedged in square, while the inside of the compartments were constructed of shoring. When they were being mined, a temporary, three-inch-thick wooden floor was constructed over the cribbing to give miners a platform to drill. In later years, an Alimak pneumatic elevator known as a raise climber was introduced to Butte in hopes of easing the difficulty of raise mining.

SLUSHER MOVING COPPER ORE. The width of the excavation indicates the vein of ore is wide. A train of cars below is loaded as the chute empties the ore. The roof is called the back. Stopes are the mined-out area between two different levels. After several feet of raise was driven and cribbed, the stope miners took over, mining horizontally from the raise but a few feet above the main level where they entered the manway. Miners climbed up the ladder and blasted into the ore, creating floors, not levels.

#5123—Butte Miner moving
copper ore with a Slusher to
open Chute .rain of EMPTY Mine
cars are loaded from Chute
mouth at Bottom of Raise

Wide exavation like this m
means that Vein of Ore was
wide. In Butte-Roof is called
back. In very early days all
this was shoved by hand

MINER MUCKING IN STOPE, C. 1900. The stopes were timbered similar to a drift, unless the ore vein was wider than six feet. If a vein was twelve feet wide, for example, the six-feet-long caps would have to be paired to allow the floors to be wide enough to extract all of the ore. Most of the time, the ore bodies had a raise on each end, and the floors were mined-out to the next raise.

46

SLUSHER PULLING ROCK THROUGH UNDERGROUND DRIFT. In the earliest days of stope mining, all of the rock was mucked into wheelbarrows and dumped down the chute. In the 1930s, the invention of the slusher made mucking easier. The slusher consisted of a double-drum winch and a bucket. The slusher block, which was a pulley-style wheel, was attached to the rock with an eye-pin. The eye-pin had a circular opening at the top and an expandable anchor shell at the bottom.

TIMBERING AN UNDERGROUND MINE, BUTTE HILL. The eye-pin was placed into a drilled hole and threaded until the shell would expand and hold it in place. A cable was strung from one of the drums, run through the eye-pin, and spliced to the back of the bucket, while the cable from the other drum was spliced to the front of the bucket.

NORTH BUTTE MINING
COMPANY SLUSHER. Rock
was slushed into the ore
chute and tumbled down to
the main level, remaining in
the chute until a motorman
or his partner, a swamper,
pulled the chutes to fill the
ore cars. Slushers varied in
sizes, and gathered anywhere
from a couple hundred
pounds of material, up to
10 tons in a single pass.
Smaller slushers were powered
pneumatically, and the bigger
ones needed to be electric.

A DANGEROUS PRACTICE, c. 1900.
A man looks up the stope while
his partner hoists timber. When
the miners had reached the next
raise, or the end of the ore body,
they returned to the manway
and up the raise to drill and blast
again horizontally. When each
floor was completely mined, the
men would move up the raise and
continue blasting, all the while
working on a three-inch-thick sill!

OPEN FLOORS IN THE STOPE, C. 1900. Some miners would double up on the three inches to ensure stability as the sill timbers were the only ones nailed in place, and a loose sill could result in a man falling through. When the stope was completely finished, it had eight-foot-tall floors for the 100–300 feet of space between the main levels.

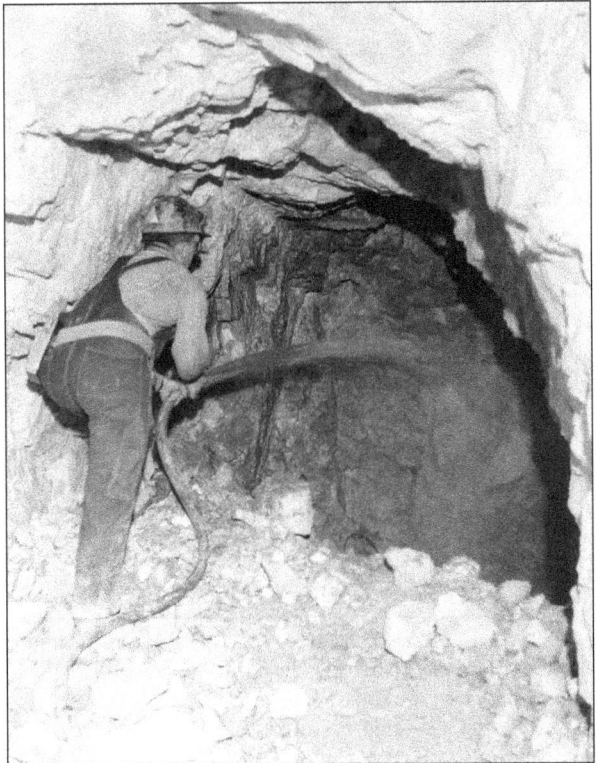

FILLING UNDERGROUND WORKINGS WITH SLIME. In the 1930s, the cut-and-fill stope was implemented. In a cut-and-fill stope, as miners advanced the floor, they would not timber the entire thing. Instead, they wedged six-by-six-inch wooden beams, known as stulls, between the foot and hanging wall. Stulling up the hanging wall would ensure more safety. After the floor was mined and stulled and all the ore had been removed, a slurry mixture of sand and water, called slime by the miners, was pumped in to fill in the floor.

ST. LAWRENCE MINE SLIME PLANT. The plant was designed to unload four railroad cars of tailings at a time with fire hoses. The tailings washed down into a large tank. Pumps would take the tailings from the tank and pump it through a wooden line to the Anaconda, St. Lawrence & Pennsylvania mine on the right. Sand for the slime was ground waste rock from the mines. The slime filled in the large voids the miners were creating.

MINER IN A GRIZZLY DRIFT. Drift and stope mining are considered narrow-vein mining. With small stringers of ore being laden through the host rock, moisture and air had the potential to work its way between the rock and ore, causing the ground to become unstable, or friable, and making it too dangerous—nearly impossible, even—to stope. Caving the entire zone was the solution. During the 1950s, at 500 feet below the surface, miners constructed a block-cave system.

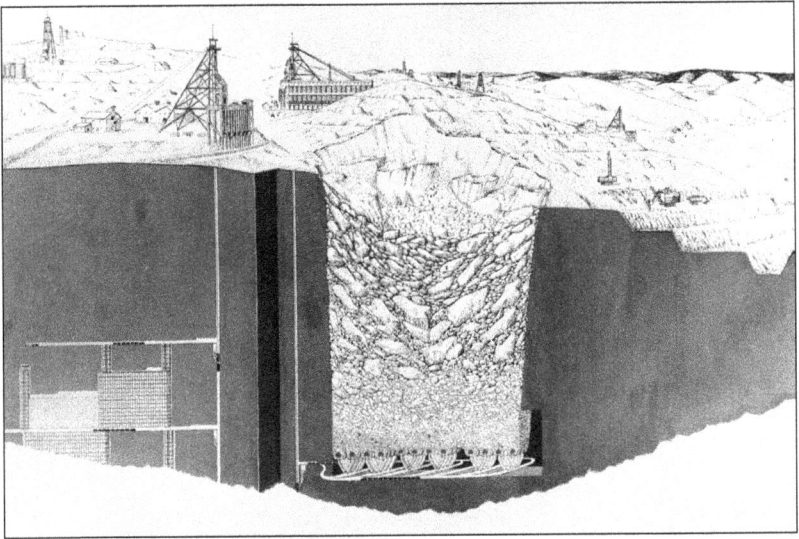

THREE TYPES OF MINING. This illustration is from Anaconda Copper Mining Company. In the center is the pick and shovel and blast method, on the left is block caving, and on the right is open-pit mining.

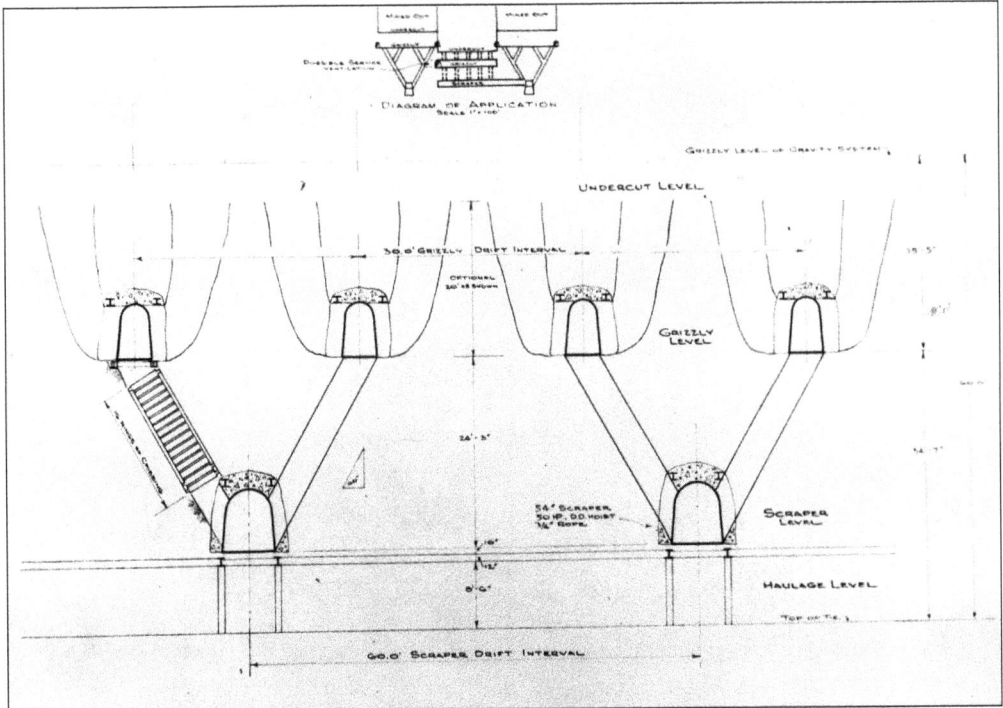

KELLY MINE BLOCK-CAVE SYSTEM. Finger raises, which are shorter raises consisting of just an ore chute, were blasted from the middle of the slusher lane up toward the friability zone. The fingers were typically two rows of three, meaning three raises on each side of the drift. Then, a large raise was driven through the middle of the zone, and eye drifts were blasted from all four sides of the raise. A miner drilled holes to the ends of the friability zone, filled the holes with explosives, and blasted. Eye drifts were only tall enough for a miner to squat through, and were spaced every 15–25 vertical feet from each other, starting from the top of the raise down toward the undercuts.

BATTERY LOCOMOTIVE IN MINE. Eventually, the entire zone started to crumble and cave. The rock that would cave from the top was so large, it fell down and inward churning the entire zone. The heavier rock from the top crushed the rock near the bottom until it was small enough to pass through the finger raises. The rock fell through the finger raises and landed into the slusher lanes, where miners operating 10-ton slushers pulled the rock into chutes to fill ore cars. The Kelley Mine had one block-cave zone 500 feet below the surface and another 1,500 feet below. Both zones were caved from the levels up to the grassroots in the topsoil. The Berkeley pit, a surface mine that excavated many of Butte's shallow veins in 1955–1982, eventually swallowed the caved zones.

ALICE MINE, WALKERVILLE MINERS, C. 1893. Butte miners were classified as days-pay and contract workers. Days-pay workers dug drainage ditches referred to as "piss ditches" by the miners; they also replaced rails, repaired timbers, operated motors, and pulled chutes. Contract miners engaged in mining, drilling, blasting, mucking, and timbering. Contract mining meant the miner was paid based on the work he had accomplished, either by the footage or cubic footage they advanced per day.

SPECULATOR MINERS BEFORE A SHIFT, 1910. Miners always worked in pairs; everyone underground had a partner to watch for and someone to watch for him. Some miners could blast multiple times during a shift, but only if they were in a secluded part of the mine. Sometimes, blasting needed to take place during a shift, usually if a boulder was lodged in the chute or pocket. Typically, a quarter, a half, or an entire stick of dynamite was needed to free the hang-up or break the rock down to a manageable size.

BARRING DOWN ON LOOSE ROCK. When a miner started his shift and arrived at his working area, there would be a muck pile left from the crew before him. There was fractured rock overhead that could slip off the back, injuring or killing the miner. So the back needed to be examined and these loose rocks pried off. A six-to-twelve-feet-long scaling bar with a chisel point on one end was stabbed at the back to remove the loose slabs. The process was known as barring down. If a loose slab could not be barred down, it was stulled up until the proper shoring could be administered. The rocks that fell from the backs of the Butte mines were called duggans after Duggan's Mortuary. When the duggan in the mine got you, Larry Duggan, the mortician, got you next. After the back was barred down, miners would remove the water lines from their drills and wet down the muck piles. After the pile was mucked, the rock was shored properly, and the miners began to drill.

54

HAND DRILLING, 2,000 LEVEL OF A BUTTE MINE. The earliest drills in the mines were the labor-intensive hand drills. It began with a single miner wielding a short-handled, four-pound hammer (known as a single jack) at a two-foot-long, chisel-pointed drill steel. After each strike, the steel was rotated a quarter turn from its position and hammered again. Periodically while drilling, the steel was removed from the hole and a long spoon was used scoop out dust from the hole. The handle of the hammer had a leather strap looped through it, which the miner would put around his wrist. That way, on his back swing, he loosened his grip and tightened it on the fore swing to hammer the steel, saving his hand muscles from cramps and fatigue. To blast a drift tall and wide enough, several holes had to be drilled; this outlined the drift for the height and width, and added several holes in the middle to break the rock into manageable pieces. By drilling with two-foot-long steel, the biggest advance a miner could make was two and half feet, unless the rock conditions were unusual and broke even further back—but that was extremely rare.

UNDERGROUND WITH CANDLES. Oil lamps were not used in the mines for fear that oil would keep burning if they were tipped or broken. The early underground miners used candles. Miners working a 12-hour shift took nine candles, eight for the shift and one extra. The candlelight dimly illuminated the work area, and in some instances, the end of the drill steel was nearly impossible for the miner to see. When double-jack drilling, one miner holding the steel would cover the batter end with his thumb, his nail giving just enough reflection for the hammerer to see where to strike. Just before the swing, by the second miner, he would move his thumb from the steel.

DRILLING HOLES, PREPARING TO BLAST. Once the holes were drilled, they were loaded with dynamite. Blasting occurred just before the miners went off their shifts. By the mid-1890s, as copper production was moving faster and faster, pneumatic drills were introduced to Butte. One of the first was a Drifter drill, nicknamed the "slugger" by some Butte miners. The drifter drill was extremely heavy and hard to move, but it still took several holes to make any advancement. As it drilled further and further, the drill had to be cranked.

CRANKED DRIFTER MACHINE, C. 1920. In most cases, the deeper the mine went, the harder the rock became. A new drill was introduced to Butte. Named for its inventor, Leyner, the drill rotated. It was set up on two metal posts similar to the slugger, however, this drill rotated the steel as it cranked forward. By the 1910s, the work in the underground mines was starting to take its toll on the miners. More and more, the miners were developing breathing, lung, and other respiratory problems. It was determined that the rock dust from the drilling was the culprit. Consequently, these drills were known as widow-makers around Butte. The solution for the rock dust was a simple as wetting it down. Drills were recalled and redesigned to push water through hollow steel, stifling the dust before it could become airborne. While the water in the drills helped offset a very real concern, it also created new ones. The water temperature in some mines was recorded to be 175 degrees, and some water spilling out of the holes while drilling appeared to be boiling.

WRONG WAY OF DRILLING. In the photograph, the drill has fallen on the miner's foot. Safety was a constant factor in the mines. Shaft miners would use sinker drills, which were later renamed jackhammers as they became popular in industries other than mining. Raise miners operated stoper drills (known as wiggle-tail drills) and buzzie drills.

STOPER DRILLING UNDERGROUND, c. 1940. The stoper was smaller and lighter, and some miners were able to muscle the stoper for use horizontally. Buzzie drills were big and bulky and were nearly impossible to drill anywhere but upwards.

58

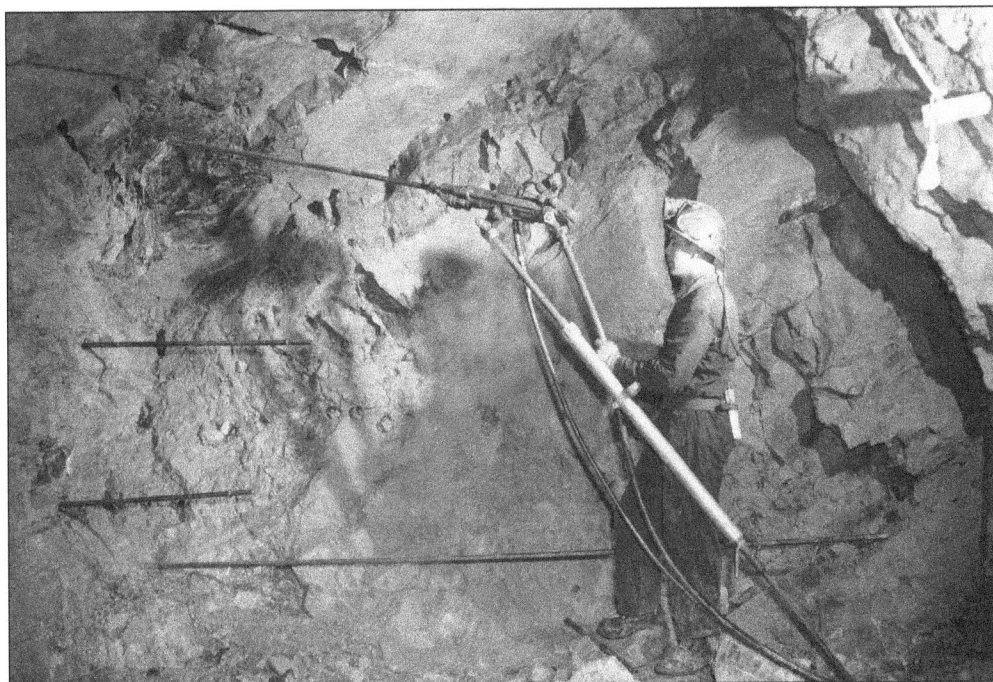

JACKLEG DRILL. The drill that revolutionized the mining industry was the jackleg. It sat on a single leg that did not have to be wedged between the back and floor; the leg had a stinger on the end that dug into the floor.

BUTTE MINER USING JACKLEG. Most jackleg drills were used for driving drifts and stopes, although some experienced miners would use them to mine raises. Jackhammers used at construction sites are pneumatic and deafeningly loud; the mining drills, slushers and mucking machines, are just as loud, but the six-by-eight-feet, hard rock hallway does not dissipate sound like the open air will. Earplugs were unheard of until the 1970s when the industrial safety movement began. Many miners suffered from hearing loss.

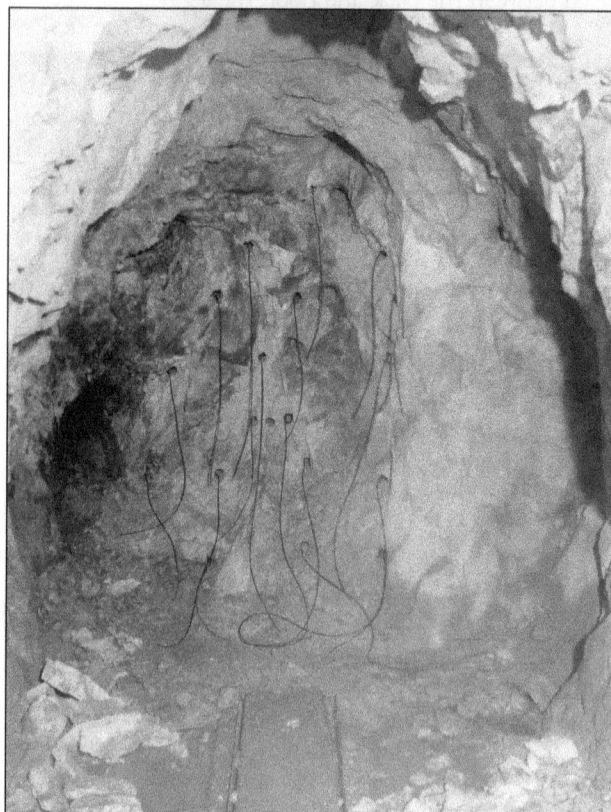

HOIST AIR COMPRESSOR.
Some mines had their own
compressors. Eventually, the
entire Butte Hill had one
central compressing plant,
but some mines were so
deep, and so many tools were
being powered that the giant
compressors were installed in
large rooms underground.

READY FOR A BLAST. While the
mining technology evolved, the
basic principles hardly varied.
Several holes were drilled into
a rock face, filled with blasting
powder, and blasted. The center
of the face was drilled with three
to nine holes several inches
apart, known as the burn. Once
the holes were drilled, the airline
was removed from the drill and
attached to a long metal tube (or
blowpipe). All water and mud
was blown out of the holes.

POWDER ROOM IN UNDERGROUND MINE.
The powder room was kept locked with
the dynamite distributed at specific times
during the mine shift. The dynamite
was fashioned into sticks without fuses
attached; to detonate the explosive, blasting
caps were needed. The men that took
care of the underground powder (blasting)
magazines were called powder monkeys.

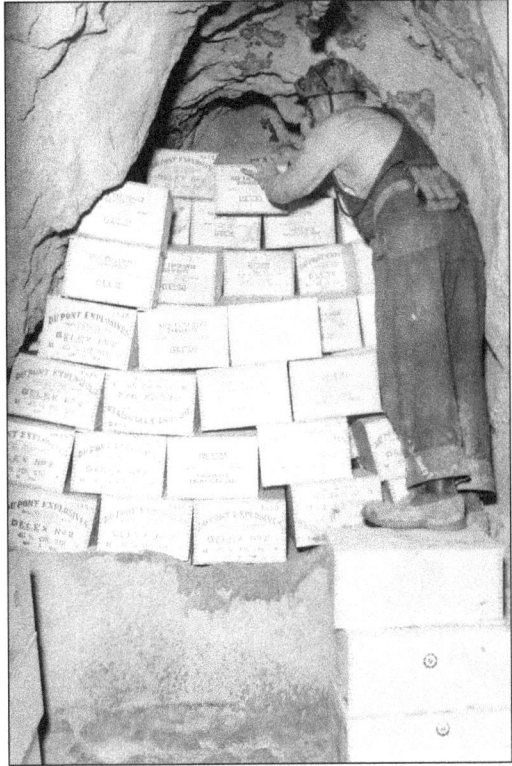

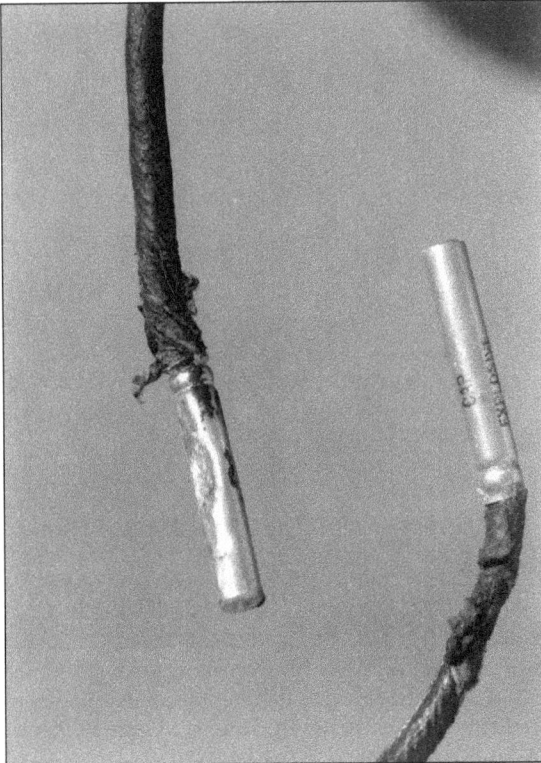

BLASTING CAPS FASTENED TO FUSE.
Caps were small, round metal tubes
that have claimed fingers and hands
when detonated prematurely. Fuses
were placed in the open end of the cap
and crimped in place. They were then
inserted into the dynamite through a
nail-punctured hole. The dynamite was
shoved into the back of the hole drilled
into the ore with long, wooden dowel.

LOADING DYNAMITE INTO DRILLED COPPER ORE. Each hole required skill in placing the sticks of dynamite. Wood was the only material that could be used to place the dynamite into the hole, as it would not generate static electricity. Each hole only had one dynamite stick with a cap; the remainder of the hole was filled with split sticks of dynamite without caps. When filling the holes with a loading stick, the popular phrase "Tap 'er light" was birthed. It was a warning that if a stick was tamped too hard, it may detonate. Today, that term is used as a way of saying good-bye in Butte

LIGHTING FUSES FOR BLAST, C. 1895. Not all drill holes had to be filled with explosives; a miner may leave one or a few holes empty. The holes needed to be timed to detonate seconds apart from each other; if all holes exploded at once, the energy created would find one void from which to escape, and the rock would not break. This is known as freezing the face.

62

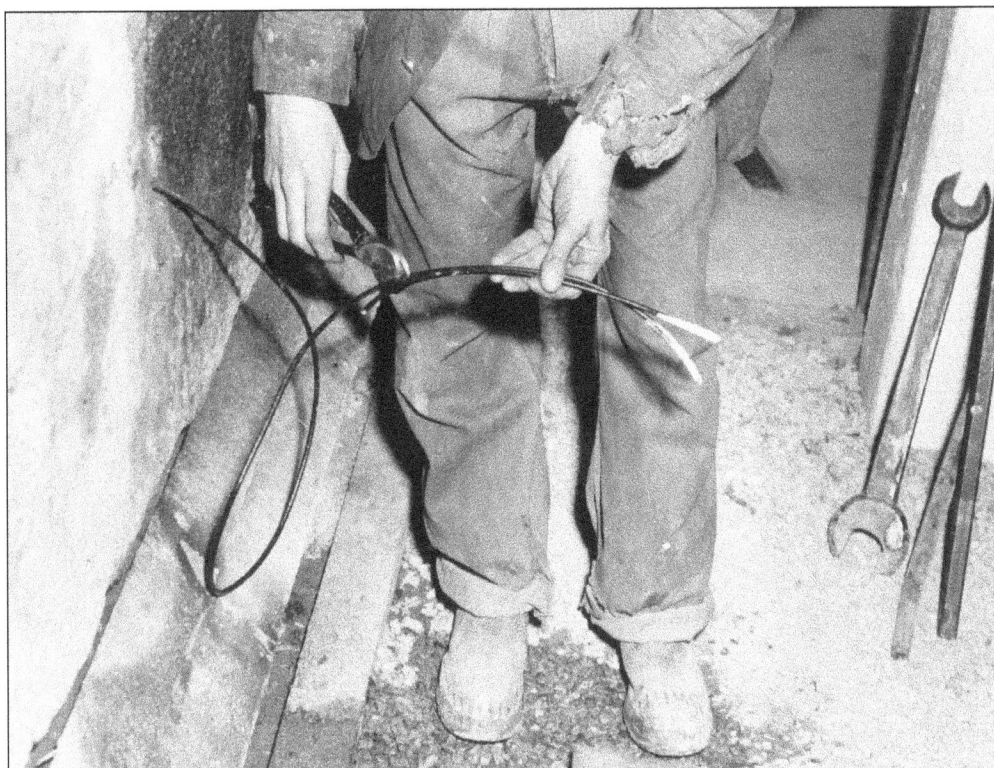

TIMING THE SHOT. Preparing the fuse before blasting rock underground is known as timing the shot. Most miners would deal with 20–30 fuses; trying to light them one at a time was both nerve-racking and dangerous. Instead, the fuses were bunched in groups of 12–15, tied together with a 2 smaller strands of fuse, and cut off square between the strands; now all the fuses could be lit at once.

UNDERGROUND POWDER MAGAZINE, SHIFT BOSS. The miners had eight to fourteen minutes to escape the blast face, as the fuse burned one foot in 38–45 seconds. Rounds were timed so that the center portion would blow out first, creating a void for other rock to break. Timing was staggered so the sides would detonate at different times: the corners were opposite from each other, the top blew before the bottom, and the bottom holes blew last.

CHECKING CAPS AND FUSES. In later years, fuses and crimping camps gave way to electric caps. They were pre-timed with indication labeled on the cord. They were wired together and detonated with a blasting box. A plunger (a spin dial that engaged to metal points), a two-button (one button for charging and the other firing), or a toggle switch was used.

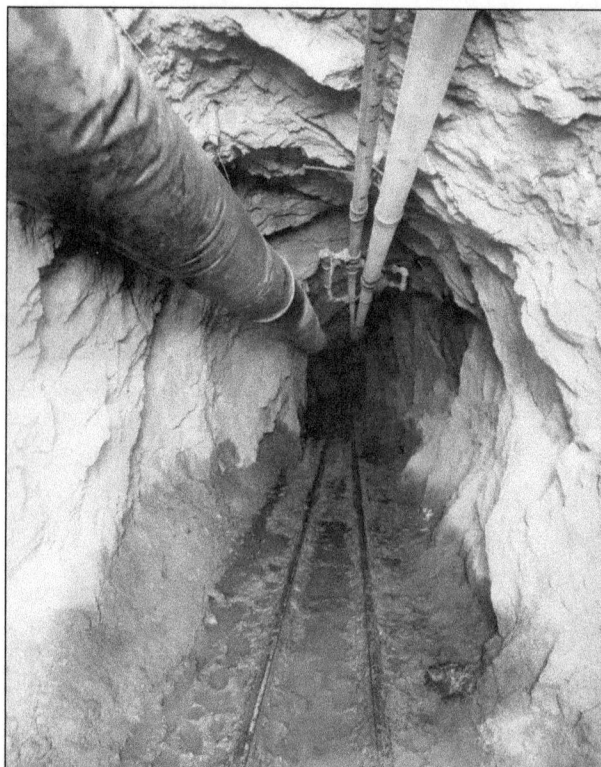

VENTILATION FAN ABOVE DRIFT. There were two common ways of ventilating the Butte mines; natural and forced-air ventilation. The shafts had downcast or up-cast airflow. Ventilation raises were raises breaking to surface or other primary shafts connected by drifts.

AIRSHAFT, GREEN MOUNTAIN MINE. The fan drew out the bad air from the mine. Fresh air was then piped into the mineshafts. If a shaft was downcast, the flow would travel down the shaft, through the haulage drifts, and up the raise or a separate shaft back to the surface. Some vent raises and shafts no longer in use were equipped with exhaust fans to enhance the ventilation and remove the smoke and fumes faster after blasts.

BUTTE UNDERGROUND VENTILATION DOOR. A compressed air cylinder opened the door. Typically, haulage drifts were the only ones naturally ventilated by the number of men passing through. But with the number of crosscut drifts branching off the haulage ways, the natural flow would lose its pressure if the crosscuts were not blocked off. Wooden air doors were constructed at the crosscut drifts, and the remaining air gaps were sprayed and filled with gunnite, a refractory material similar to stucco. Some air doors were opened and closed using an air piston; others were opened manually.

FRESH AIR, MOUNTAIN CONSOLIDATED MINE. Beyond the air doors, miners would need a way to breathe. Electric fans ranging from one to six feet in diameter were installed, and canvas tubes of the same diameter (known as vent or fan bags) were added to the fans. Being made of canvas, extensions to the bag could easily be made as the drifts, stopes, and raises were expanded, while the fan stayed in one place. Some areas in the mines were so hot; miners would climb inside of the bags, several times during their shifts, trying to cool off. Some places were so violently hot that cooling systems were installed near the fans. Some miners said the coolers made the conditions hot enough to work. As the mines were expanded down and out, underground streams, springs, and aquifers were constantly being crossed, sometimes flooding areas. The mines had to be dewatered, or the entire operation could fill highly acidic mine water.

READING TO BLAST BERKELEY PIT, C. 1966. The last mine to close in Butte was the Kelley in 1979. The nearby Berkeley pit saw its last shift in 1982, and with no income to pay the power bills the Kelley pumps were shut off. The Berkeley pit, only 1,200 feet deep from its lowest point and 1,600 feet deep from its highest, began taking on the acidic mine water as early as 1985. This meant that all the underground mines of Butte were flooding just the same. The Berkeley pit is now Montana's deepest lake, over 1,000 feet deep—and the world's largest contaminated body of water. The water adds stability to underground Butte, as most of the workings are completely shored up by timbers, and because the timbers are completely submerged, no air can rot them. The copper water does not eat the timbers like it does metals.

BROTHERHOOD. After years of mining, it did not matter from where a partner hailed; they relied upon each other once they descended into the mines. Labor strikes were common, and martial law was brought to Butte twice. Unions were built in Butte with much hard work and danger, at times. The history of unionizing the miners involved the dynamiting of the union hall, the lynching of an union organizer, and shootings. But Butte was, and still is, a community of friendship and brotherhood. During strikes, shop owners would give families materials on credit, knowing they would square up the bill once work resumed. Miners worked hard and played harder; gambling was common, and bars and saloons were open 24 hours a day to accommodate for the around-the-clock work in the mines.

Two

THE MINES

UPPER WEST SIDE WITH MISSOULA MINE, C. 1970. The mines covered the Butte Hill. At the time of World War I, there were over 400 mines on the hill. Small mines started and stopped, but the major mines operated for years. This section contains just some of the mines that operated in Butte. Today, there are a handful of headframes still dotting the Butte landscape. There were over 450 mines located in Butte. The mines ranged from the large operations to the very small, which may have only been diggings or which operated for very short time. The mines evolved from the early enclosed headframes to the construction of steel headframes as mining progressed. The varied names of the mines reflect the rich diversity of people who started the mines. Many of the origins of the mine names are lost today

BELL MINE AND TIMBER YARD. The Bell mine was owned by the Anaconda Copper Mining Company in 1900. The shaft was 1,800 feet deep, and 275 men were employed at the mine. The Bell Mine was one of many mines named honoring women. The Bell Mine was first named Belle, after a belle of the early mining camp. The mine later came to be known as the Bell-Diamond Mine.

THE TRAVONA MINE. This was a silver and manganese mine around 1950. In 1874, William Farlin started the mine, which he named the Asteroid Mine. This mine produced hundreds of thousands of dollars of silver and later manganese. When copper king William A. Clark acquired the mine, he changed the name to the Travona Mine, after a province in the Balkans.

THE PARROT MINE. The steel headframe was moved to the Neversweat mine in 1915. The final shaft was 2,800 feet deep. The mine was part of the group started by James Ramsdell, an early Butte mining pioneer.

THE NETTIE MINE. This mine was located west of the Orphan Girl Mine. Little is recorded about the Nettie Mine. Like many mines in Butte, the origin of the name is a mystery today, lost to time.

MAIN RANGE MINE. This mine was located in the McQueen Addition in Butte and was 2,200 feet deep. It was owned by North Butte Mining Company. There is a copper mining area in Michigan named the Main Range.

ST. LAWRENCE NO. 7 MINE. The St. Lawrence mine was named for the home county of Edward and Michael Hickey, early Butte miners, who heralded from St. Lawrence County, New York. Michael Hickey made the discovery that laid the foundation for the Anaconda Company. His claim was named the Anaconda. The shaft was 600 feet deep.

PAYMASTER MINE. The Paymaster Mine was located north of Main Street in Walkerville. The Alice Mine is at the top of the photograph with the four tall stacks.

NIAGRA MINE. The Niagra Mine was located below the Black Rock Mine dump in Butte.

NEVERSWEAT MINE. The photograph shows the Neversweat Mine above the area known as Dublin Gulch. This area was home to many of the Irish of Butte. This mine was distinguished by its seven stacks, which could be seen throughout Butte. It was one of the original mines purchased by copper king Marcus Daly.

LITTLE ELM ORLU MINE. The Little Elm Orlu Mine was located in the Black Rock No. 1 mine yard in Butte. This mine belonged to Copper king William A. Clark. There was also an Elm Orlu Mining Company.

ELM ORLU MINE. This manganese and silver mine was north of the Badger Mine. The mine was part of William A. Clark's holdings at one time. The shaft was 3,469 feet deep.

BLACK ROCK NOS. 2 AND 3 SHAFTS. The Butte & Superior Mining Company is just starting to sink these mines, known as Black Rock No. 2 and No. 3 shafts. This was the only mine in Butte that had a separate chippie shaft until the Kelley Mine was developed. The No. 2 shaft was 3,000 feet deep, and the No. 3 was 3,600 feet deep.

THE BUFFALO MINE IN CENTERVILLE. From left to right are Old Glory Mine, Corra Mine, Buffalo Mine, Diamond Mine, Mountain Con No.1 Mine, and Mountain Con No. 2 Mine around 1915. In 1900, the Anaconda Company owned the mine. It was 1,600 feet deep and employed 100 men.

HEADFRAMES OF KELLEY MINES NOS. 1, 2, AND 3. This view looks to the south of Butte around 1953. The chippie cage at the Kelley Mine could hold 104 men and two decks. The Kelley Mine was part of the Anaconda Mining Company's Greater Butte Project, which included the Kelley Mine, the Ryan Mine, and the Leonard Mine. They were to be the three main company operations in Butte. This project never came to completion.

BALAKLAVA MINE IN MEADERVILLE. This mine was located just east of Butte. In 1953, the shaft was 1,600 feet deep. The mine was named for a famous battle where the Light Brigade so valiantly charged. The related word *balaclava* is knit cap that covers the head and neck.

BELL-DIAMOND MINE WITH ORE BINS. The Diamond Mine was owned by the Anaconda Copper Mining Company in 1900. At that time, the shaft was 2,200 feet deep, and the mine employed 550 men. By the end of mining here, the shaft was 3,500 feet deep.

NEW STEEL HEADFRAME AND ENGINE ROOM. The Mountain Con's headframe and engine room were photographed after completion around 1928. In 1900, the Anaconda Company owned the mine. It was 2,000 feet deep and employed 550 men. This was a copper mine with tons of copper hauled from its depths. In later years, it was said to be a mile high and a mile deep. The final shaft was 5,390 feet deep.

ALICE MINE, C. 1930s. Marcus Daly managed the mine for the Walker Brothers. Located in Walkerville, this was the first mine project for Daly in Butte. The mine was a large silver producer, and a mill was located at the mine. It was open-pit mined in later years.

PENNSYLVANIA MINE, EAST BROADWAY STREET. The Belmont Mine is on the far left. Just below the Belmont is the small headframe of the Lucky Jim Mine owned by the Boston and Montana Company. In 1900, the shaft was 1,430 feet deep, and 300 men were employed at the mine.

TUOLUMNE MINE. This mine was later converted to an airshaft. It was one of the early Butte mines.

PITTSMONT NO. 4 MINE. This mine was owned by the East Butte Mining Company, as were the Pittsmont Nos. 1, 2, and 3 Mines. This complex has miners' boarding houses located at the mine. The distance from the main center of Butte necessitated housing at the site. The final shaft was 2,600 feet deep.

PITTSMONT NO. 3 MINE. The Pittsmont complex was located in East Butte, which was a large mine area. The shaft was 1,200 feet deep.

PITTSMONT NO. 2 MINE. The Pittsmont No. 1 Mine. This was next to the Pittsmont No. 1 Mine and Smelter. The shaft was 1,800 feet deep.

BADGER STATE MINE, C. 1928. When it closed in 1966, this mineshaft at the end on Anaconda Road was 4,169 feet deep. The mine was started in 1883, and the headframe is still standing today. It was principally a copper mine.

MOOSE MINE AIRSHAFT, C. 1950. In 1900, the mine was owned by the Boston and Montana Company. It was 300 feet deep and employed 30 men. The mine was named after the animal. Many mines bore names of animals, such as the Buffalo Mine and the Badger Mine.

REINS MINE. The Reins Mine was located on Main Street in Meaderville. It was the airshaft for the Leonard Mine, which was also called the Betsey Dahl and the Combination. The building on the right with the long roof was the Rocky Mountain Cafe. The headframe in the background on the left is the East Colusa Mine.

NEW HEADFRAME, BERKELEY MINE. The workers are installing a new wooden headframe. The large headframe came from the Rarus Mine. The original headframe is underneath the new one. The mine was owned by the Butte and Boston Mining Company in 1900. The shaft was 700 feet deep, and there were 70 men employed at the mine.

ANSELMO MINE HEADFRAME. Erected on December 15, 1936, the headframe came from the Black Rock Mine. The mine began mining zinc, and later in the year, copper was mined. The Anselmo Mine yard still stands in Butte today. It contains many of the buildings used when the mine operated. When the mine closed, the shaft was 4,301 feet deep.

GEM MINE. Pictured is the East Gem shaft of the North Butte Mining Company. The Gem Mine was under lease to Allan Hooper & Associates in 1955. The Speculator and Diamond Mines can be seen in background. This headframe is located at the Lexington Garden in Butte today.

WEST COLUSA MINE, JUNE 1902. The chippie cage was large enough to fit a horse standing up. This mine in Meaderville was part of the Boston and Montana Mining Company. The mine was 1,370 feet deep and employed 175 men. The final shaft was 3,200 feet deep.

LEONARD MINE NO. 1 SHAFT.
In 1904, the Leonard No. 1 shaft
was sunk in Meaderville. The
mine was part of the Boston
and Montana Company mining
group. The main Leonard shaft
was 1,130 feet deep and 180 men
were employed at the mine. The
final shaft was 2,200 feet deep.

COLORADO MINE. The mine is shown with a steel headframe. The headframe was moved to the
Orphan Girl Mine when the Colorado mine was closed in 1925. The mine's name came from
the home state of its founder. The shaft was 3,400 feet deep.

SMOKE HOUSE MINE. The Smoke House Mine was located at the corner of Broadway and Wyoming Streets. The Thornton Building is in the background. There are multiple stories as to how this mine acquired its name. One story says that an ore vein near the surface was discovered when a cigar store called the Smokehouse was torn down to make way for a new hotel. Once the ore was discovered, the hotel development was abandoned, and the mine was started.

CORA MINE. Pictured in the center of the photograph, the Cora mine was owned by the Montana Ore Purchasing Company in 1900, a company owned by copper king Augustus Heinze. The shaft was 400 feet deep and employed 50 men. The final shaft was 2,800 feet deep.

PITTSMONT MINE NO. 1. The Butte and Boston Smelter is in the background. The Rarus Mine is at left, on the hill.

DIAMOND MINE. This mine was located on the top of the hill overlooking Butte. It was part of the Mountain Consolidated Group acquired by the Anaconda Copper Mining Company. Principal mines in this group included the Modoc Mine, the High Ore Mine, the Green Mountain Mine, the Mat Mine, and the Mountain Con Mine.

EMMA MINE. It was located three blocks below Park Street. Like many mines, this one was named after a woman, either a wife or sweetheart of the mine locator. Besides the Emma Mine, lines bearing female names included the Nettie Mine, the Minnie Jane Mine, the Minnie Healy Mine, and many others.

FLAG FLIES AT ANACONDA MINE. It was the first mine owned by the Anaconda Copper Mining Company. The shaft was 1,800 feet deep, and in 1900, it employed 1,400 men. The final shaft depth was 3,800 feet.

HIGH ORE MINE. In the background, from left to right, are the East Gray Rock, the Corra, and the Bell Mines. The tunnel under the headframe in the bottom right of photograph was used for ore train loading. The mine was named for the high-grade ore discovery at the mine's start. At the turn of the century, the mine was owned by the Anaconda Copper Mining Company. Its shaft went 2,200 feet deep, and 300 men were employed at the mine.

THE RARUS MINE, C. 1910. The mine belonged to copper king Augustus Heinze. In 1900 the mine was owned by the Montana Ore Producing Company. The mineshaft was 1,100 feet deep and 250 men were employed at the mine. The final shaft depth was 3,900 feet.

MORE THAN SPECULATION, C. 1910. The Speculator Mine was named by Pat Largey Sr. He considered his claim at its beginning to be a speculation. In 1900, the mineshaft was 1,200 feet deep, and 70 men were employed. The final shaft depth was 3,400 feet.

SEVERAL BUTTE MINES, C. 1910. The Speculator Mine appears with the Tuolumne, Ticon, Diamond, and Jessie, Mines c. 1910. The Speculator mine was the site of the 1917 mining disaster resulting from a fire in the mine.

NEVER OPENED, C. 1950. The Ryan Mine North of Walkerville belonged to the Anaconda Copper Mining Company and was never put into operation. This was a temporary wood structure for sinking a shaft. A new hoist and steel headframe were onsite but not installed.

TWO BLACK ROCK MINESHAFTS, C. 1920. On the left is the No. 1 shaft, and on the right is the No. 3 shaft. The No. 3 headframe was moved to the Anselmo Mine in the 1930s.

MINING STREET SCENE. A streetcar is heading east on West Daly Street in Walkerville, just east of Excelsior Avenue. The Moulton and Alice Mines are on the left, followed next by Magna Carta Mine, Valdamere Mine, and the Lexington Mine and Mill. The Lexington Mine was named after the historic American Revolution battle.

THE CHINESE LAUNDRY. The Steward Mine is located on the east side of North Main Street, just North of Woolman Street in uptown Butte. The Steward Mine shaft was 1,100 feet deep at the turn of the century, and it employed 200 men. The mine was named for the man who discovered it. The mine was known as a hot uncomfortable mine to work in. It was often referred to as the Chinese Laundry.

A Busy Place. The Granite Mountain Mine owned by the North Butte Mining Company was located west of North Meaderville.

Parnell Mine. The Parnell Mine was one of the many mines that bore an Irish name. Note the cement plates in the center of the mine yard. They were used in an experimental airshaft lining. The plan was not successful because the plates came loose and fell. Other mines shown are the Anaconda Mine (left) and the Neversweat Mine. In 1900, the mineshaft was 700 feet deep, and 35 men were employed there at the mine.

MODOC MINE. The headframe was used for sinking a circular shaft for an airshaft in the early 1960s. Around 1900, the mine was owned by the Anaconda Copper Mining Company. The shaft was 1,100 feet deep, and the mine employed 100 men. The final shaft depth was 2,800 feet.

TWO MORE UNIQUE NAMES. Looking west from above Walkerville, the Blue Wing Mine is on the left and the Casper Mine is on the right.

MOONLIGHT MINE. It was located on East Granite Street. In 1900, the mine was owned by the Anaconda Copper Mining Company. It had a shaft 1,500 feet deep and employed 350 men.

ORIGINAL AND GAGNON MINES. Located on North Main Street in uptown Butte, the Gagnon Mine had an incline shaft around 1935. The Original Mine, also located on North Main, was so-named because one of the first mine lodes in Butte was recorded there in 1864. In 1900, the Original shaft was 1,300 feet deep, and 200 men were employed. The Gagnon shaft was 1,800 feet deep and employed 300 men at this same time.

WALKERVILLE MINES, 1937. At the top of photograph are the Moulton (left) and Alice Mines. Below the Alice Mine is the Bell of Butte Mine.

HEADFRAME UNDERWATER ABROAD. The Sarsfield Mine headframe was originally at the Speculator Mine. It was later moved from the Sarsfield Mine to Chile, South America, and dropped in the bay where it still is today.

PILOT BUTTE MINE, C. 1918. The Elm Orlu Mine dump appears on the left and the Butte and Superior Company Black Rock Mine in the background. The wood headframe of the Pilot Butte Mine is still standing today.

MAKING WAY FOR THE PIT. The Mountain View Mine is being dismantled as preparations are being made for the opening of the Berkeley pit. The mine was once called the Saffron Bun Mine. This mine occupied a prominent view atop the Butte Hill and was subsequently named Mountain View Mine. At the turn of the century, the shaft at the mine was 1,750 feet deep, and 125 men were employed at the mine.

STREETCAR JUNCTION. The streetcar tracks branched off from the Columbia Gardens tracks near the Old Silver Bow Mine airshaft. The Silver Bow Mine No. 1 has the largest, widest stack. Below it is the Silver Bow No. 2 Mine. Both mines were owned by the Butte and Boston Mining Company in 1900. The Silver Bow No. 1 Mine had a shaft 1,000 feet deep, and it employed 185 men. The Silver Bow No. 3 Mine shaft was 500 feet deep, and 50 men were employed there.

WALKERVILLE

MINE, MILL, AND SCHOOL, C. 1890. The Moulton Mine and Mill in Walkerville is pictured in the upper right of the photograph. In center is the Bell of Butte Mine, and to the far left is the Sherman School.

LITTLE MINAH MINE, 1880S. The mine was located in Centerville just below the Mountain Con Mine. This was one of the many mines named for wives or sweethearts of the mine locators.

MOUNTAIN CON MINE NO. 2, C. 1880S. During the time the photograph was taken, this Centerville mine went to a depth of 1,800 feet underground and employed approximately 300 men. Its weekly output was 2,500 tons. The Mountain Con No. 1 Mine is in the background.

POULIN MINE, CENTERVILLE. In the 1880s, it was a Washoe property, and at one time, production was temporarily stopped to await completion of the Anaconda Smelter in Anaconda, Montana.

BULK-BLOCK CAVING. In 1900, the Adams Mine was owned by the Anaconda Company. The shaft was 1,200 feet deep and employed 100 men. The mine was located near the Mountain View Mine.

WEST GRAY ROCK MINE. Located just west of the Diamond Mine, West Gray Rock was originally owned by James King. Con Kelley's father, Jerry Kelley, was the manager. In 1900, the mine was owned by the Butte and Boston Company. The shaft was 700 feet deep, and the mine employed 50 men.

A NAME FROM NEVADA. The Ophir Mine was located just off South Montana Street by the railroad tracks. The mine's name came from the Ophir Mine in Nevada City, which was owned by the Washoe Gold and Silver Mining Company No 1. The company was formed by George Hearst, who was involved in mining interests with Marcus Daly.

EAST GRAY ROCK MINE. This mine was located adjacent to the Diamond Mine yard. In 1900, the mine was owned by the Butte and Boston Company. The shaft was 1,800 feet deep, and 150 men were employed at the mine.

NEW LEONARD MINE HEADFRAME. Workers are installing a new headframe in 1942. The small headframe underneath was not taken down; it stayed in place until the newer steel headframe was moved to the Kelley Mine around 1950.

BLACK ROCK NO. 1 MINE, C. 1910. The mine was located north of Meaderville. Note the lumber in the timber yard at the lower right of the photograph. The shaft was 2,000 feet deep.

EAST COLUSA MINE. The East Colusa Mine in Meaderville was owned by the Boston and Montana Mining Company. Its shaft was 800 feet deep and 65 miners were employed there around 1900. Copper ore came to the surface at 3 or 4 locations east of the mine where it was mined at the Colusa pit. The shaft was 3,800 feet deep.

103

RAMPART MOUNTAIN, EAST OF McQUEEN. From left to right are Butte and London Mine, Green Leaf Mine, North Butte Extension Mine, Main Range Mine, Pittsmont No. 3 Mine, and Pittsmont Smelter.

EAST RIDGE, NORTHEAST MEADERVILLE. From left to right, at the center of picture are Boston and Montana Hospital, Six O'clock Mine, Butte and London Mine, and Green Leaf Mine. In the foreground is the North Butte Extension Mine.

SILVER KING MINES NO. 1 AND NO. 2. These mines were located near the 400 block of Quartz Street in Butte. The mine on the left had an incline shaft. Most mines on the Butte Hill had vertical shafts.

NAMED BY THE IRISH, C. 1900. Parnell Mine in is in the foreground and Hungry Hill is in the background. The Hungry Hill area of Butte was named by the Irish after their homeland in Ireland.

SILVER BOW NO. 3 MINE. This mine was located on Butte's East Side. The photograph shows the mine with an enclosed headframe. Fires eliminated the use of the enclosed headframes by the turn of the century.

COLORADO MINE, EAST PARK STREET. The wood headframe pictured was later replaced by a steel headframe. The steel headframe went to the Orphan Girl Mine in 1925. The Orphan Girl Mine is the home of the World Museum of Mining today.

EAST STEWARD MINE, ANACONDA ROAD. The headframe was enclosed. This mine had an incline shaft. The majority of shafts in Butte were vertical.

ANOTHER VIEW. The headframe of the East Steward Mine at the time of this photograph was enclosed. They stopped using enclosed headframes at the turn of century because they were a fire hazard and replaced them with open headframes.

COOLING AIR CURRENTS, C. 1900s. The Ramsdell Parrot (foreground) and the Neversweat (background) Mines were owned by the Anaconda Copper Mining Company in 1900. The Neversweat Mine was named due to the unusual air currents, which kept the mine cooler than other underground mines at the time. The Neversweat mineshaft was 2,000 feet deep, and the mine employed 600 men. The Ramsdell Parrot Mine shaft was 600 feet deep, and this mine employed 200 men.

MINE LITIGATION. This view from the 1900s shows the Minnie Healy Mine in Meaderville with the East Colusa Mine on the right. At the turn of the century, the Minnie Healy was owned by the Montana Ore Producing Company. There were 150 men employed at that time, and the shaft was 1,800 feet deep. This mine was involved in the Apex Litigation cases involving Augustus Heinze.

PILOT BUTTE MINE. It was located below the Badger Mine. Black Rock Mine is visible on the left in the background. The shaft was 2,800 feet deep.

RIGHT BOWER MINE, C. 1940s. The Right Bower Mine was located in North Meaderville and was 500 feet deep. In later years, it was used as an airshaft.

THE THREE PARROT MINES. Shown is the Colusa Parrot Mine with Neversweat Mine in the background. In 1900, the mineshaft was 1,600 feet deep, and 350 men were employed. This mine was owned by W.A. Clark. There were three mines in this complex the Parrot Mine, the Colusa Parrot Mine, and the Ramsdell Parrot Mine.

NIPPER MINES NO. 1 AND No 2. The Neversweat Mine is in the rear, and the Anaconda Mine is to the left. Dublin Gulch is in the foreground. The Nipper Mine had a shaft 800 feet deep, and 150 men were employed at the mine in 1900. This mine was owned by Augustus Heinze.

PAYMASTER MINE. The mine origin of the mine name is not known. It is believed that the dream of wealth from the mine played a part in its naming. It was a smaller mines on the hill.

HEADERVILLE ...nard Mine   Aug 2nd 1937   Leonard Min
Butte, Montana

ACCIDENT AT LEONARD MINE. This incident occurred when the hoisting engineer forgot to reverse the hoisting engine. The engine's power, plus the weight of a loaded skip cage on the 3,300-foot level, pulled the skip over the sheave wheel and broke the steel hoisting cable.

TRAMWAY MINE. This mine was an early mine owned by Augustus Heinze. It was part of his Montana Ore Purchasing Company, which he later sold. Where the mine acquired its name is lost to history. This headframe was moved to the Kelley Mine in 1952 for the chippy frame.

EARLY MINES, C. 1890. Early mines of Butte included, from right to left, the Parrot Mine, the Neversweat Mine with its seven stacks, the East Steward Mine, the Nipper No. 1 Mine, and the East Minah Mine. Mines spanned across the Butte Hill with housing for the miners built next to the mines.

112

Three

THE PEOPLE

NOT A TYPICAL MINING COMMUNITY. This view looking up north Main Street toward the Lexington mine in Walkerville shows the Mountain Con Mine on the right. Butte was not a typical mining community. Mark Twain had once visited and was shocked to see the miners dressed dapperly, rather than in their diggers. All of Butte's mines were connected by drifts; miners could descend the furthest east shaft, and surface from the furthest west shaft and never see the light of day during the trip. Butte had over 400 mines. So if a miner quit or was fired from his mine, he could pack up his turkey, walk across the street, and rustle work at a different mine. A turkey was a burlap sack miners would carry their diggers, boots, hardhat, and tools in when moving from mine to mine. Butte was home to many demographics, the majority Irish. A close second were the Cornish or Italians, and workers came to Butte from 30 other nations as well. Different nationalities lived in their own neighborhoods, and some mines would only hire specific heritages, but feuding and discrimination was short-lived.

COVERED IN MUD. Mine safety was an important concern in the mines, and these company officials are dressed to inspect the underground mine workings. They are covered in mud form their trip into the mines. Ed Renouard is on the far right. Over 2,500 men died in the Butte mines.

NO HARDHATS, YET. This photograph was taken around 1913 at the Mountain Con Mine, which was said to be a mile high and a mile deep. The miners are dressed in their work clothes. Note the lack of hardhats. At the time of this photograph, miners still used candles for light underground. The hardhats held the carbide lamps for light in later days.

MANNING THE CHIPPIE HOIST.
The Badger State Mine's chippie
hoist hauled the miners up and
down the shaft. One story for its
name is it ran around constantly
hauling miners, reminding them of
wanton women known as chippies.
The round dial behind the miners
noted the level of the cage.

NIGHT SHIFT CREW. This photograph of workers at Badger Mine in Walkerville was taken November 16, 1945. Mine employees included, from left to right, (first row) Reddy Rock, Dinny Lynch, Tucker Cook, Bill Berryman, Bill Farnum (Dutch), unidentified, Alec Siladi, Woody Schrader, Bill Baron, unidentified, and Bob Christenson; (second row) unidentified, John Tomazich, Ted Davis, Andy Hislop, Les Williams, Joe Panion, Jocko Giacamino, Stan Benny, unidentified, and Mickey Ryan; (third row) Frank Cavley, Jim Malloy, Jim Kertin, Steve Art Carline, Al Maunder, Jim Champion, Clarence Hibbs, Otto Nelson, and Lawrence Mansanti; (fourth row) Percy Tretheway, John Niemi, George Hollings, unidentified, Stewart Branner, ? Patty, Jerry Lowney; (fifth row) "Socho" Jack Stevens, Tom Coyle, Tom Murray, Talmer "Brick" Dennehy, unidentified, Alec McInnes, unidentified, Mike Kinney, and Jack Holland.

BELL-DIAMOND MINE OFFICIALS. Standing second from left is M.J. Burke, third from left is Tom Walker, and seated second from right is Mr. Hogue. Early on, most large mines had their own office and payroll departments. Later, as mines became part of larger groups, these functions were consolidated.

LUNCHTIME. These carpenters are eating lunch at the Mountain View Mine with a dog in the foreground of the photograph. Many of the large mines had carpenter shops. The carpenters made everything out of wood the miners needed.

116

FIRST AID TEAM, TRAMWAY
MINE. The teams held first aid
competitions at the Columbia
Gardens each year. Members of
this team are, from left to right,
(first row) John Everest, John
Rowe, and Jim Michelotti; (second
row) Adolph Ossello, Julius
Casagrande, Andrew Antonovich,
and Bill Marsh.

DESPERATION AIRSHAFT. The
shaftman is standing in the
sinking cage for the Anselmo Mine
desperation airshaft in Butte. It was
an up-cast shaft. This equipment
was removed after a shaft was
sunk. This shaft was on Excelsior
Avenue and Caledonia Street.

A SPECIAL TOUR. Pictured are a group of women touring a Butte mine at the 1,500-foot level. Tours were conducted at the mines on special occasions. Visiting groups found the mines an interesting experience.

1500 LEVEL

NEW EQUIPMENT. Green Mountain Mine in Centerville has just received three new boilers. The boilers are still crated, as seen in the center of the photograph behind the group of miners. These boilers were used with the steam hoists. In later years, this mine was used as an airshaft for the Mountain Con Mine.

A Big Crowd. W.A. Clark's Famous Fraction Mine adjoined the Alice Mine on the east side of Walkerville. The people in the photograph are not miners as noted by their clothing. This photograph was taken when William Jennings Bryant visited Walkerville.

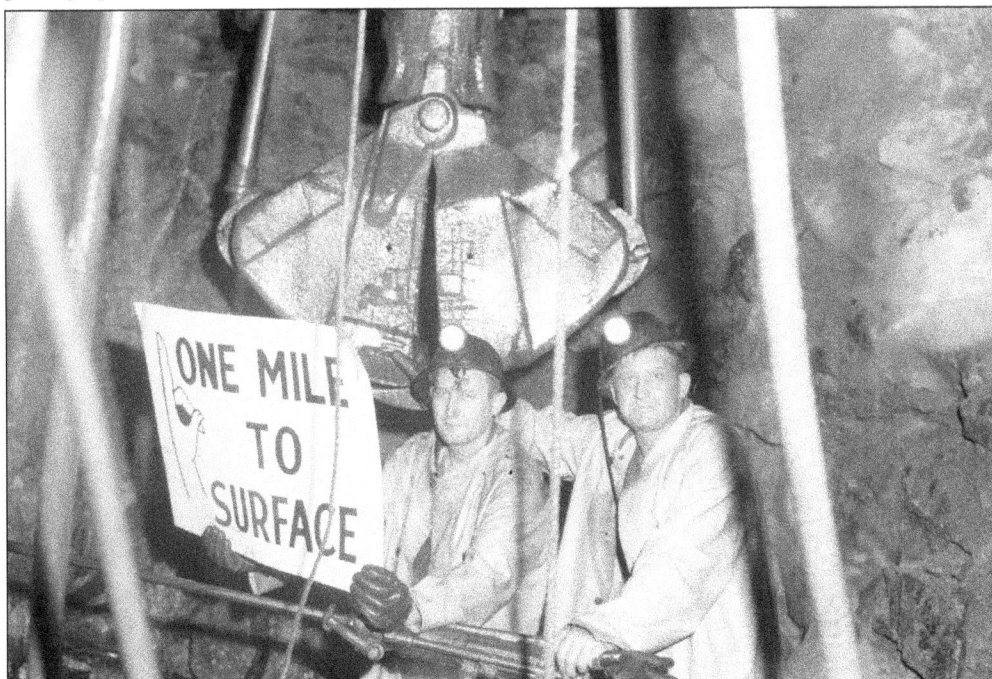

One Mile to Surface. The Mountain Con mineshaft mine was 5,390 feet deep, the deepest of all Butte Mines. It stood at an elevation of 6,135 feet. The mine was started in 1890 and closed in 1974. Larry Lammi (left) and Morris Hanninen (right) are pictured in the shaft.

Large Group of Early Miners. This picture was taken by Jeremiah Crowley from County Cork, Ireland, while visiting a Butte mine. Note the candles, which provided the only light in the mines at this time.

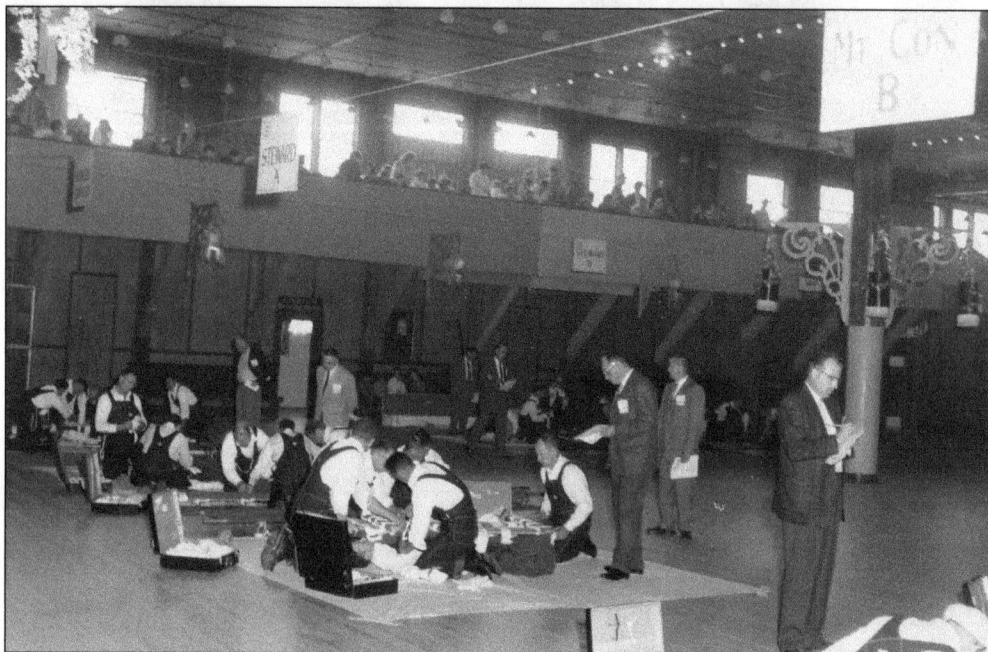

Columbia Gardens. The dance hall at the Columbia Gardens is where the first aid teams from the Butte mines competed every Miner's Union Day. Each mine had first aid teams equipped to handle all injuries and accidents, from the most severe to the simplest injury.

A FAMILY AFFAIR. Six sets of father-and-son pumpmen teams are pictured with one boss at High Ore Mine. Some of the other workers at the mines were swampers, who served as brakemen and often loaded the mine cars; blacksmiths and blacksmiths' helpers, who sharpened tools and did forging, welding, and other blacksmith work; and boilermakers and helpers, who did all the electric and gas welding, repairing, and servicing on the surface and in the mines.

THE MULLANEYS, HIGH ORE MINE. Pumpman Jerry Mullaney is pictured with sons Jim (left) and Tom (right). Some of the other occupations at the mines included pipemen-surface, men who took care of all water, steam, and compressed air lines on the surface; machinists and machinist's helpers, men who took care of and installed the machinery above and below ground; and drymen, who cleaned and took care of the Dry (change house), usually older miners nearing retirement.

121

THE COMBOS, HIGH ORE MINE. Pictured are father and son, Robert Combo Sr. and Robert Jr. Other mine workers would have included samplers, who went underground and take ore samples so that miners can be advised which rock was pay ore and which was waste; mine surface crew, who unloaded the railroad cars of timber; and powder monkeys, who took care of the underground powder (blasting) magazines.

THE BENNETS, HIGH ORE MINE. These pumpmen are pictured with the father and son team of Paul and Joe Bennet. Others working at the mines included repair men, miners that were constantly replacing broken mine sets of timber and making other repairs underground, usually days-pay employees; miners, who do all the underground mine excavating, including drilling, blasting, and timbering, often on contract; and hoisting engineers, who worked in eight-hour shifts around the clock.

THE DAVISES, HIGH ORE MINE. Pictured are pumpmen and father and son, Terry and Frank Davis. Some of the other occupations at the mines included oilers, who oiled the hoisting engine, kept the engine room clean, and learned to operate the hoist; topmen, who usually worked in pairs loading and unloading the cages; and station tenders who also usually worked in pairs. They rode the cages when empty and loaded and unloaded the cages at the various levels in the mine. They received 50¢, more than days-pay miners.

HARD ROCK. Gary Brookins is pictured at Leonard Mine's mucking machine around 1950. Good miners are very skilled in their work, and in the Butte mines the term *hard rock* is a good descriptor. Miners are classified as driftmen, who drive the drifts and crosscuts (tunnels) into the earth, raise miners, who handled work on the raises, and stope miners who worked on the stopes where the ore was mined.

In the photo, handwritten labels appear: "Boss Boss", "TARZAN", "FOR MAN", and along the bottom: "A.C.M." "BLACKSMITHS" "Butte mine shop"

BLACKSMITH SHOP, PARROT MINE YARD. The blacksmiths did all the metal work at the mines. They built the cages that went up and down the shaft. Most large mines had their own blacksmith shops.

GROUP OF MINERS, NATIONAL MINE. The mine was located on North Montana Street below Nanny Goat Hill. The mine companies took photographs such as these showing shifts of miners. Unfortunately the names were not recorded for history.

124

BUTTE MINES

Adelaide

Adirondack

Agnostic Claim

Alex Scott

Alice

Alice-Lexington Tunnel

Alliance

Allie Brown

Altona

Amadore

Amy

Anaconda

Anderson

Anderson Lode

Angela

Anglo-Saxon

Annear

Annex Plummer

Annie & Oda

Anselmo

Antonioli

Apex

Aplite

Ardsley

Artic

Ash Tunnel

Atlantic No .1

Atlantic No. 2

Atlantic No. 3

Atlantic Shaft

Azor

Badger State

Balaklava

Balm

Baltic No. 2

Baltic No. 3

Bannister

Barnard

Batchelor

Belindia

Bell

Bell East

Belle of Butte

Bellona

Belmont

Benham

Berkeley

Berlin

Bertrand Lessee

Betsey Dahl

Big Bonanza

Black Rock No. 1

Black Rock No. 2

Black Rock No. 3

Blind Jack

Blue Bird

Blue Jay

Blue Wing Shaft

Blue X

Bob Ingersoll

Boehme

Bonanza

Boston Shaft

Boston Tunnel

Brazil

Brewer Claim

Bricker

Britania

Buffalo

Buffalo West

Bullwacker

Butte & London

Butte Copper Czar

Butte Milwaukee

Butte-Boston

Butte-Duluth

Butte-New England

Calumet

Cambers

Carrie

Chapman

Charmer

Chief Joseph

Childe Harold No. 2

Cima

Clark-East

Clark Tunnel

Clark's Fraction

Clear Grit

Colorado

Colorado-Leon

Extension

Colorado-Parrot

Colusa

Comanche

Copper Glance

Copper Zar

Corra

Corra No. 2

Cripple

Cripple

Croesus

Darling

Davis

Dead Horse

Deadman

Destroying Angel

Destroying Angel Tunnel

Dewey Tunnel

Diamond

Ding Bat

Discovery

Discovery Shaft

Discovery Tunnel

Dixon Lease

Dolan

Double

Dutton

Eagle Bird Claim

East Butte

East Butte Extension

East Butte Extension No. 2

East Butte No. 5

East Butte No. 6

East Butte No. 7

East Butte No. 9

East Colusa

East Gray Rock

Edith May

Elba

Ella

Ellingwood Shaft

Elm Orlu

Emily

Emily Tunnel No. 1

Emma

Estella

Eveline

Farlin

Farrel

Flat Iron

Frank Moulton

Fredonia

Gagnon

Gallatin

Gambetta

Gambrinus

Gambrinus No. 1

Gambrinus No. 2

Gambrinus No. 3

Garfield

Garibaldi

Gem East

Gem West

Germania

Geyman

Giant

Ginsberg

Gladstone

Gladstone No. 2

Glengarry

Gold Hill

Gold Hill No. 2

Golden Rule

Goldsmith

Goldsmith

Goldsmith No. 2

Gopher

Granite Mountain

Grant Extension

Gray Eagle East No. 3

Great Republic Claim

Green Copper Disc

Green Leaf

Green Mountain

Grimes

Groeneveld

Ground Squirrel No. 1

Ground Squirrel No. 2

Gypsy

H&W

Hancock

Handlin

Harris

Hatty

Hay

Heaney

Helen Blazes

Henry George

Hibernia

Hickey

High Ore

Holbrook

Homestake

Hornett

Hoskins

Hoy

Humbolt

Humbolt Lode

Idaho

Idle Wild

Iduna

Isele Butte

Ivey

J.I.C.

James

Jasper

Jennie Dell

Jersey Blue Shaft

Jessie

Josephine

Kane No. 1

Kane No. 2

Kane No. 3

Kelley No. 1.

Kelley No. 2

Kelley No. 3

Kemper

Kennedy

Kessler

Klondike

L.E.R.

La Plata

Late Acquisition

Late Acquisition No. 1

Leaser's

Leaser's Shaft

Leaser's Shaft No. 5

Leaser's Shaft No. 6

Leggat & Foster No. 2

Leonard No. 1

Leonard No. 2

Lesse Tunnel

Lessee

Lewisohn

Lexiington

Lexington

Lexington North

Liquidator
Little Annie Shaft
Little Darling
Little Gold Hill
Little Mina
Little Mina East
Little Sarah Claim
Lizzie
Lucky Jim
Lucky Seven
Lynch
Macawber
Maggie
Magna Charta
Magnolia
Main Range
Mapleton Claim
Margaret Ann
Marquis
Mary Louise No. 1
Mary Louise No. 2
Mary Maclane
Matt
May Shaft
Mcbarron
McDonald
McGowan
Mcintyre
Micheal Devitt
Midnight
Mill Tunnel
Milwaukee
Minnie Healy
Minnie Healy
Discovery Shaft
Minnie Irvine
Minnie Jane No. 2
Minnie Jane No. 4
Missing Link
Missoula
Missoula
Missoula No. 2
Missoula No. 3
Mitchell
Modoc
Modoc Extension
Modoc Extension Shaft
Modoc West
Molly Murphy
Monitor
Monitor Tunnel
Moonlight
Moonlight South

Moonlight Tunnel
Moose
Moose No. 3
Morley
Morning Star
Morning Star East
Moscow
Moulton
Mount Moriah
No. 2
Mountain Boy
Mountain Chief
Mountain Con
Mountain
Con No. 1
Mountain
Con No. 2
Mountain View
Mountain View
Airshaft
Mullins
Murphy
National
Neptune
Nettie
Nettie No. 2
Neva
Neversweat
New Era
New Era No. 1
New Era No. 3
New Sutton
Niagara
Nipper
Nipper No. 2
Non-Consolidated
Non-Such Fraction
Nora
North Butte
Extension
North Pole
North Star
Northey Shaft
Norwich
Oden No. 2
Old Bell
Old Glory
Old Glory West
Olive Branch
Oneida
Ophir
Ora Butte
Original

Original No. 6
Orphan Boy
Orphan Girl
Otisco
Otisco No. 2
Otisco No. 3
Pacific
Parnell
Parrot
Pat Wall
Paymaster
Pearce
Pearce Lease Tunnel
Pennsylvania
Penoa
Penrose Shaft
Pershing Tunnel
Peters
Pilot Butte
Pilot Butte
Pilot Shaft
Pittsmont
Pittsmont No 2
Pittsmont No 4
Pittsmont No. 1
Pittsmont No. 3
Plymouth
Plymouth Discovery
Poser
Poser No. 3 Tunnel
Poser Surface Tunnel
Poser Tunnel
Poultin
Preferencia
Prospector
Pyle No. 10
Pyle No. 2
Pyle No. 3
Rainbow
Ramsdell
Ramsdell Parrot
Rarus No. 1
Rarus No. 2
Ravin
Raymond
Raymond Tunnel
Reins
Rialto
Richard-Moulder
Right Bower
Rising Star
Robert Emmett
Rock Island

Rose
Rose O'Malley
Ryan
Sankey
Sarsfield
Saul
Shakespear
Shannon
Shonbar
Showne
Silver Bow No. 1
Silver Bow No. 2
Silver Bow No. 3
Silver Bow West
Silver Cleft
Silver King
Silver King No. 5
Silver Queen
Silver Safe
Silversmith
Sinbad
Sioux Chief
Sirius
Sister
Smoke House
Snohomish
Soudan
South
Speculator
Spence
Spruce
Spur Claim
St. Lawrence
St. Lawrence E. E. Line
St. Lawrence No. 2
St. Lawrence No. 7
Stanislas
Star West
Stella
Steward
Steward East
Steward East Old
Sullivan
Sunny Dell
Sutton
Syndicate
Tecumseh
Tension
Thomas No. 1
Thomas No. 2
Three Eleven
Ticon
Tiger Claim

Tom Gray
Torrid
Tramway No. 1
Tramway No. 3
Tramway No. 4
Travona
Travonia
Trerise
Trifle
Tripod
Tropic
Tuolumne
Tzarena
Tzarena Tunnel
Valdemere
Vanzandt
Venus Claim
Veronica
Veronica Rep
Virginius No. 1
Virginius No. 2
Volunteer
Vulcan
Wake Up Jim
Walker
Walkerville Claim
Wappelo
Washoe
Wedge
West
West Colusa
West Gagnon No. 2
West Gray Rock
West Lake
West Mapleton
Whim
Wightman
Wild Bill
Windlass
Wolcat
Wollman
Wolvin Tunnel
Wyoming St.
Yankee Boy
Yellow Jacket
Zella

The World Museum of Mining (WMM) was founded in 1963 by the hard work and commitment of the Butte Exchange Club and individuals who realized the importance of preserving Butte's mining and cultural heritage. They had the foresight to recognize that Butte's future residents and visitors would seek knowledge of the intricate workings of the mines and the people who contributed to this era in America's history.

The economy of Butte was changing, moving from deep underground mining to large-scale open-pit mining. This shift meant neighborhoods and underground mines would be swallowed up by the open pit mining, leaving no trace of the substantial cultural and historical aspects of the community. The Exchange Club identified the danger of losing resources that interpreted Butte's and the region's past. They convinced the Anaconda Mining Company (ACM), who was the holder of the vast mining properties spread throughout the area, to donate the Orphan Girl mining property for the purpose of establishing a place of preservation for cultural and historical artifacts.

The mission statement of the World Museum of Mining was developed and still clearly describes its purpose and intent:

The mission of the World Museum of Mining is to preserve the rich historical legacy of mining and the related culture of Butte, Montana, and the surrounding region and to promote the significant mining heritage by educating the public with a perspective toward total family interest.

Currently, staff and volunteers forge ahead with the ideals that shaped the museum and work diligently to continue to tell the story of an internationally renowned city that produced fabulous fortunes from its mines and also to honor the descendants of a melting pot of cultures whose pride in their heritage and traditions is evident, even today.

WORLD MUSEUM OF MINING
155 Museum Way
PO Box 33
Butte, Montana 59701
www.miningtmuseum.org
406-723-7211

Visit us at
arcadiapublishing.com

....